TIME FOR DINNER

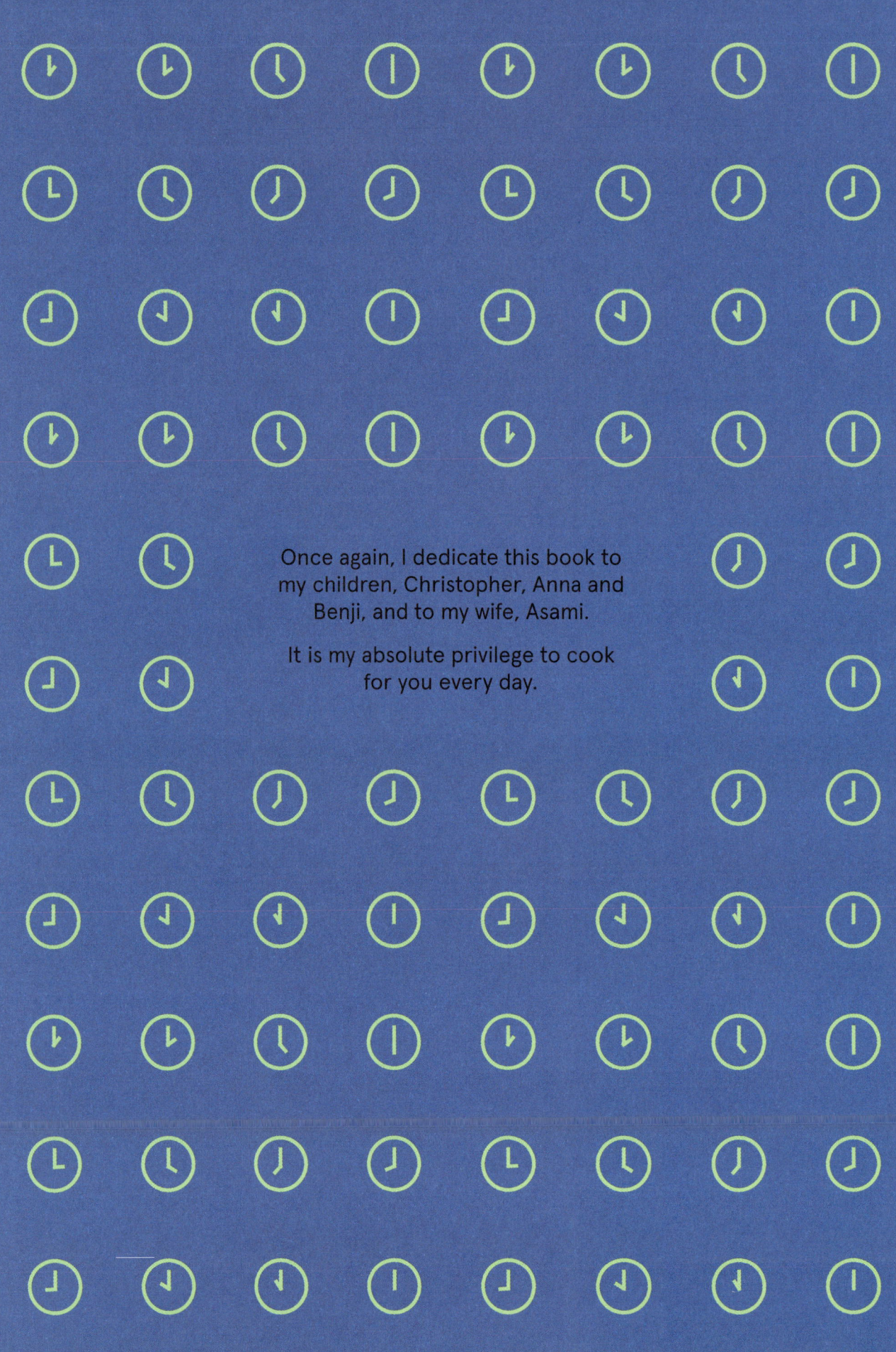

Once again, I dedicate this book to my children, Christopher, Anna and Benji, and to my wife, Asami.

It is my absolute privilege to cook for you every day.

TIME FOR DINNER

SMARTER RECIPES FOR FASTER COOKING

ADAM LIAW

Hardie Grant

BOOKS

6	INTRODUCTION
12	HOMEMADE CONVENIENCES
14	25 TIME-SAVING TIPS

UNDER 10s

22	SALAD LYONNAISE
25	TOMATO TARTINE
26	CURRIED EGG FURIKAKE
29	THE ORIGINAL CAESAR SALAD
30	BOMBAY CHEESE TOAST
33	CARBONARA FRIED RICE
34	FISHERMAN'S LUNCH
37	ASSIETTE DE CRUDITÉS
39	DAKOS TOAST
40	BLUE CHEESE AND GREEN APPLE SALAD

LESS TIME SHOPPING

46	KIDNEY BEAN CURRY
48	LITTLE FRENCH PEAS
51	KERALA EGG CURRY
53	CARROT AND GREEN BEAN STEW
54	ALOO MATAR WITH BROWN BUTTER TADKA
57	KIMCHI AND GARLIC BUTTER FRIED RICE
59	FROZEN PEA SOUP WITH BACON AND CORN CROUTONS
60	TAMAGO-DON
63	EDAMAME SUCCOTASH
64	RICOTTA EGGS ON TOAST

LESS TIME CHOPPING

71	FROZEN VEGETABLE FRIED RICE
73	ROAST PUMPKIN WITH TAHINI SAUCE
74	RUMP CAP WITH QUICK CHIMICHURRI
77	TURKISH TANDOORI DRUMSTICKS
78	BEEF TAGLIATA
80	SWEDISH MINCE
83	SAUSAGES IN CIDER AND MUSTARD
85	TWICE-ROASTED POTATOES
86	CHEESEBURGER SANG CHOY BAO
88	GARLIC CHICKEN DRUMSTICKS
91	LAMB KHEEMA

LESS TIME COOKING

96	PRAWN AND LEMON GUAZZETTO
98	QUICK CHICKEN NOODLES
101	SALMON WITH PARSLEY AND DILL SAUCE
103	PAN-ROASTED FLATHEAD WITH PEAS, GREENS AND BACON
104	CRUMBED CHICKEN TENDERS WITH PESTO MAYONNAISE
107	QUICK DUCK À L'ORANGE WITH SARLADAISE POTATOES
109	SPANISH GARLIC PRAWNS
111	STEAMED FLATHEAD WITH SPINACH AND LEMON SAUCE
112	BARBECUED SQUID WITH OREGANO AND PAPRIKA
115	QUICK SRI LANKAN PRAWN CURRY

LESS TIME WASHING

- 120 MANGALOREAN PORK MASALA
- 122 ORANGE AND FENNEL CHICKEN TRAYBAKE
- 125 COLCANNON RISOTTO
- 127 BAKED TUSCAN CHICKEN
- 129 TURKISH ROAST LAMB SHOULDER
- 130 CREAMY CHICKEN, LEEK AND MUSHROOM STEW
- 133 MUSHROOM CACCIATORE
- 134 HONEY MUSTARD CHICKEN CUTLETS
- 137 WHOLE BAKED FISH WITH VADOUVAN BUTTER
- 138 SOY SAUCE CHICKEN WITH SPRING ONION OIL
- 141 HAWAIIAN SHOYU CHICKEN

WHILE THE PASTA COOKS

- 146 TOMATO AND CAPSICUM PENNE
- 149 PACCHERI WITH PANCETTA AND PISTACHIO
- 151 SPAGHETTI VONGOLE ROSSO
- 152 CHICKEN AND CREAM CHEESE PENNE
- 155 TINNED FISH WITH CAPERS AND TOMATO SPAGHETTI
- 157 LINGUINE WITH MUSSELS AND PANCETTA
- 158 PASTA ALLA CARLOFORTINA
- 161 'ANTIPASTA'
- 162 PANTRY PASTA
- 165 CREAMY LEMON PASTA

QUICK WOKS

- 171 PRAWNS AND EGGS
- 172 SHANGHAI SHREDDED PORK AND CABBAGE
- 175 THREE-CUP CHICKEN
- 177 BEEF PAD PRIK KHING
- 178 CHICKEN AND SNOW PEAS WITH OYSTER SAUCE
- 181 SEAFOOD YAKISOBA
- 183 CHICKEN AND CHOY SUM
- 184 FRIED EGGS AND SOY SAUCE
- 187 BEEF, ASPARAGUS AND CAPSICUM
- 189 STIR-FRIED PORK AND FENNEL
- 190 BEEF PAD SEE EW

QUICK SWEETS

- 196 CHOCOLATE GRANITA
- 199 WEET-BIX MILLE-FEUILLE
- 201 SCRAMBLED PANCAKES
- 202 MASALA CHAI
- 205 DECAFFOGATO
- 207 BAKED RICE PUDDING WITH PLUM JAM
- 208 APRICOT AND SOUR CREAM FOOL
- 210 SUPER-SOFT CHOCOLATE MUG CAKE
- 212 TOAST SUNDAE
- 215 ANYTIME CHOCOLATE AND ALMOND COOKIES

- 216 INDEX
- 222 ABOUT ADAM
- 223 THANK YOU

INTRODUCTION

THE FIRST THING I WOULD SAY TO PEOPLE WHO WANT TO REDUCE THE AMOUNT OF TIME THEY SPEND COOKING IS: DON'T.

We can all list a million things we think we don't have time for: exercising, relaxing, cleaning the bathroom or mowing the lawn. The thing is, we all feel busy. We all feel like we're time-poor. It's a sad symptom of modern life that we've been conditioned to think that we don't have time to do … well, anything.

This constant feeling of time pressure is a symptom of a world that is always trying to sell us something. The message is always, 'You don't have time, so buy this thing that will give it back to you.' It's a lie.

Spending time with our families, exercising, cleaning and cooking aren't luxuries we don't have time for. They're necessities. Imagine for a moment we really didn't have time for these things. Our relationships and our health would suffer unimaginably. That's certainly not a life that I would want.

THE CASE FOR COOKING

Food is one of the great pleasures of life. Not just eating a delicious meal, but finding ingredients, preparing them with care and, yes, even the cleaning up. Our most treasured moments with our loved ones often take place over a meal. The food we eat connects us to place, culture and the people around us.

In every civilisation in human history, food has been central to culture. The multiple harvest festivals that underpin our special occasions today were all about the collection and production of ingredients. Major events are celebrated with feasting, from birthday cakes to Christmas dinners.

If I had to choose between Michelin-starred restaurant dinners every night for the rest of my life or home-cooked meals at my dining table, there'd be no contest. (It's the home-cooked meals for me, in case you're not sure.)

Don't get me wrong. I'm not some lunatic who spends their day spinning around the kitchen filled with joy in a *Sound of Music* fever dream. Cooking can feel like a chore sometimes, but the benefits far, far outweigh the negatives.

REAL COOKING IS FAST

I have a busy life. Like many people, I struggle to achieve the right balance between work, family and personal time. I am no believer in hustle culture, 'the grind' or trying to fit more hours in the day, but one thing that gives me comfort is the truth that we will always find time for the things we prioritise.

Thankfully, cooking is fast.

Before the industrial revolution, the only restaurants that existed were attached to hotels or rest houses. They were for travellers who couldn't cook. The idea of going out for a meal when you could cook one at home was entirely alien. Sadly, industrial economics has developed in such a way that we are more valuable to the economy if we work for money and then spend that money on another person (or a factory) cooking for us rather than simply cooking for ourselves.

I don't know about you, but I don't think of myself as simply an economic unit. I'd rather spend 20 minutes cooking for my family than work for a couple of hours to make enough money to pay someone to spend 20 minutes cooking for my family. Think about how the maths of your average delivery order works out for you after tax and you'll see what I mean.

The marketing myths surrounding processed convenience foods and delivery services would have us believe that cooking food is difficult and time-consuming. Of course they'd say that. Their entire business model is to get you to pay them to do something instead of doing it yourself.

Real cooking isn't anywhere near as time-consuming or difficult as they'd have us believe.

FORGET 'RESTAURANT QUALITY'

That the term 'restaurant quality' ever became aspirational for home cooks borders on the ridiculous. The majority of meals I cook at home are far and away better than I'd be confident of getting in most restaurants around the world, but that's entirely by the by.

If you say you want 'restaurant quality' food at home, what does that even mean? To me, a good home cook will always be able to produce something better for a nightly meal than a restaurant. Restaurant cooking and home cooking are entirely different things, and one shouldn't really aspire to be the other. You could even say they're opposites: dishes in restaurants tend to be for special occasions, whereas home cooking is food for every day.

Restaurant food apportions most of its time to preparation so that food can be finished quickly à la minute when a customer orders. Home cooking generally doesn't have time for lengthy preparations. A restaurant is focused on turning a profit. At home, the economics of ingredients and labour are very different. A restaurant doesn't expect you to eat their food every day, and so health is not a primary concern. At home, health should be at the forefront of all your food decisions.

STRIKING A BALANCE

It might sound like I'm knocking the things that make nightly dinners more convenient, but I'm really not. I'm not some health influencer asking you to never touch another convenience food again. On the contrary, I have plenty of them in my fridge, freezer and pantry. They play a valuable role in modern cooking.

I eat convenience foods. I get takeaway. I go out to eat at restaurants. I enjoy all these things. But problems arise when we get the balance wrong, and sometimes we don't notice until it's too late.

I have three main problems with processed and takeaway convenience foods.

Firstly, for the most part they don't prioritise your health – the more processed foods you eat, the worse your health outcomes will be. This is a truth that scientists and health professionals shout from the rooftops every day, but we've become numb to it. Many processed foods are high in salt and sugar – and not because it makes them taste better. It's simply to improve their shelf life. The longer a product can stay on the shelf, the more money it can make.

Secondly, convenience foods are economically out of sync with how we should be eating. Processed convenience foods can often seem cheap, but put them in context – they're all about volume. Large volumes of low-quality, low-nutrient ingredients is precisely the opposite of how I think we should be eating: less food, but better.

And this brings me to my third point, and my main gripe with so many convenience foods: they just don't taste very good. A homemade hamburger made from fresh ingredients tastes better than a frozen one that has been designed to live in the freezer for months. Homemade biscuits will always taste better than biscuits that are made and sold purely for profit.

It is absolutely possible to make quick meals that are nutritious and also taste delicious. In fact, it's not just possible – it's what normal cooking was for centuries.

This is a book about fast, convenient cooking, but it's also about good cooking.

RETHINKING GOOD COOKING, FAST

I feel like we've got the whole idea of quick cooking inside out and upside down. We've been so misinformed by the convenience industry that many of us no longer know what's actually difficult and what's not. We spend a lot of time talking about ingredient lists, cooking time or preparation time, but that's only part of the story.

If a 12-ingredient dish contains eight spices that all come out of one container, does that mean it takes a long time to cook? If a lamb shoulder that cooks for 4 hours on a Sunday afternoon only takes 5 minutes to get in the oven, does that really take up a lot of your time?

The entire process that we call 'cooking' is made up of a lot of different parts. It starts when we gather our ingredients and only finishes when we're done cleaning up.

In this book, I've tried to break down the entire cooking process into different areas where you can save time. Shopping, chopping, cooking and cleaning are all part and parcel of cooking, and they're all opportunities to save a few minutes – or even more.

Under 10s includes dishes that are super quick no matter how you approach them, for those times when you're really on the clock. They all take less than 10 minutes from start to finish. From simple salads and egg dishes to clever toast toppings, I want you to rethink how quick dinner can really be.

In **Less Time Shopping** you'll find recipes you can make from ingredients you probably already have in your pantry, fridge or freezer. Eggs, frozen peas, tinned tomatoes – these are trusted and loved staples for a reason, and if they save you a trip to the shops, all the better.

Often the part of cooking that takes the most time is the peeling, slicing and dicing. In **Less Time Chopping** you'll find recipes that don't require a lot of knife work, using ingredients such as mince, sausages, drumsticks and steaks.

Less Time Cooking focuses on ingredients that cook in shorter times. Instead of slow braises and stews, there are dishes using seafood, vegetables and fast-cooking cuts, such as chicken tenderloins.

In **Less Time Washing** there are traybakes and dishes you can make in one pan or one pot. They might take a little longer in the oven, but that's time you don't need to be in the kitchen, freeing you up to do what you like.

Pasta is a home-cooking staple, but a three-hour bolognese with eight different vegetables to chop isn't exactly a quick weeknight meal. **While the Pasta Cooks** is a chapter that does exactly what it says on the box and gives you dishes you can whip up in the time it takes you to boil the pasta.

Wok cooking is my go-to quick-dinner solution, but we often overcomplicate our stir-fries to the point where they're no longer quick and nearly impossible to fry well. In **Quick Woks** I want you to keep your stir-frying simple. Trust me, you won't regret it.

Of course, no meal is complete without something special at the end. **Quick Sweets** isn't about big cakes and decadent desserts: we're talking treats that are small, quick to prepare and just the right way to finish sweetly.

STICK WITH IT

In this book I've tried to give you as many different tools, tips and ideas as I can to find recipes, techniques and workflows that fit with your kitchen and your lifestyle. Not every single one of them will be right for you, but I'm certain a lot of them will be – some might even be complete gamechangers.

My last piece of advice: stick with it. The first time you try a recipe will always be the most difficult attempt. You're looking at the book every few minutes, unsure about which pots or pans to use, and second-guessing every move you make. But if it tastes good please make it again. The second time you make it you'll halve the amount of time you spend on it and it'll taste better. The third time you make it you'll halve the time again and it'll taste even better again. Cooking is like any other skill – you improve every time you do it.

I hope this book gets you thinking about food a little differently. I hope you get some great ideas to take the stress out of preparing your nightly meals, and I hope you'll come to see that fast food doesn't have to mean processed foods, expensive takeaways or low-quality ingredients. Mostly, I hope you'll understand that cooking has value, and the time we spend on it – whether a little or a lot – is far more important than simply getting a meal on the table.

HOMEMADE CONVENIENCES

I COMPLETELY UNDERSTAND THE ALLURE OF CONVENIENCE FOODS. WHO DOESN'T WANT THINGS TO BE A BIT MORE CONVENIENT? THIS WHOLE BOOK IS ABOUT MAKING YOUR COOKING MORE CONVENIENT.

My issue with a lot of convenience foods isn't the convenience – it's the quality. They just don't taste very good. Something you make yourself will always taste better than something you buy from a shop, not least because it will be distinctive and made to your tastes.

Who would you rather be responsible for how your food tastes: a boffin in a lab formulating a shelf-stable salad dressing that can be produced as cheaply as possible, or you in your kitchen making something that tastes great from good ingredients?

Wherever you see the (⚡) symbol in this book, that recipe (or part of a recipe) can help you save time in the kitchen. Keep a little spring onion oil on hand or lo sui in the freezer, and they'll be the key to jump-starting any dinner without compromising on flavour – all from homemade ingredients and all as conveniently as possible.

CURRIED FURIKAKE   26

Although furikake is considered a rice seasoning in Japan, try it with eggs as in Curried egg furikake (page 26) or season chicken or fish before or after they hit the frying pan. Mix it with yoghurt to marinate meat or seafood as a kind of quick tandoori, or even just sprinkle it over some oven fries or Twice-roasted potatoes (page 85).

BASIC VINAIGRETTE   37

Everyone should know how to make a basic vinaigrette, and not just because most store-bought dressings are terrible. You can easily change up a vinaigrette by playing with the basic ingredients: use grapeseed oil instead of olive, or add a dash of hazelnut; replace the white-wine vinegar with cabernet, apple-cider or coconut vinegar. Otherwise, add herbs, roasted garlic or fruit juices.

QUICK CHIMICHURRI   74

Chimichurri's wheelhouse is the barbecue. Steaks, chops, sausages – it goes with all of it. You could also try it with a roast chicken (homemade or store-bought), a nice piece of grilled fish or a few peeled prawns. Honestly, there's not a lot that it doesn't go well with.

TWICE-ROASTED POTATOES   85

Keep these potatoes in the freezer after the first roasting as a great shortcut to amazingly convenient roast potatoes. First, freeze them on a tray, then transfer them to a zip-lock bag. You can give them their second roasting straight from the freezer or add them to the base of the tray when you're roasting a chicken.

VADOUVAN CURRY POWDER   137

Homemade curry powder is always a good idea. Use it in any recipe that calls for curry powder, or any roughly similar recipe that calls for a mix of spices. Try it as a replacement for the spices in Aloo matar with brown butter tadka (page 54), Lamb kheema (page 91) or Quick Sri Lankan prawn curry (page 115).

SOY SAUCE BRAISE (LO SUI)   138

This braising liquid can be used to poach chicken, pork or boiled eggs using the same method as in Soy sauce chicken with spring onion oil (page 138) – just re-season it with salt, soy sauce or sugar every few uses. You can use lo sui with beef, lamb or fish as well, but because they have a stronger aroma take some of the liquid and cook them separately.

SPRING ONION OIL   138

This oil goes with everything. Try it with a bit of steamed or poached fish, or some grilled or boiled pork belly. It's perfect with chicken of all varieties. You could even mix it with some chicken thighs and steam everything together. Try it stirred through noodles with a bit of oyster sauce, or as a dressing for bashed cucumbers.

SMOKED PAPRIKA OIL   146

This is an excellent finishing oil for almost any tomato-based pasta or risotto – just pour it on top to add a bit of smoky complexity. But don't stop there. You can use it over barbecued prawns (shrimp) or grilled squid, or as a dressing oil for steak or lamb chops. Imagine it over a Caprese salad.

YAKISOBA SAUCE   181

Don't limit yourself to noodles – this simple stir-fry sauce can be used to season anything that goes in a wok. Try it with wok-fried chicken and vegetables. You can drizzle it over okonomiyaki or even have it with a schnitzel or katsu with a bit of shredded cabbage on the side.

CANTONESE SWEET SOY SAUCE   184

I love this sauce drizzled over fried salmon fillets and as a dressing for whole steamed fish. It's great with heavier meats, too – try it on Cantonese-style barbecued pork, as a tare (sauce) for a sliced wagyu steak donburi, or over a piece of pan-fried duck breast. You can use it to season stir-fries as well.

MUG CAKE MIXTURE   210

This perfect shortcut dessert can be adapted in a few different ways. Add a spoonful of peanut butter, jam or marmalade to the mug. If you're adding peanut butter, sprinkle some nuts over the ice cream on top. Make it with coffee instead of hot water for a mocha version.

ANYTIME CHOCOLATE AND ALMOND COOKIES   215

The variations on these cookies are nearly endless. Add different chocolates, nuts or even marshmallows. Try them with dried fruits or ground spices like cinnamon, clove or ginger.

25 TIME-SAVING TIPS

SHOPPING

1. **ORGANISE YOUR PANTRY.**

   My pantry staples will be different from yours, but understanding what you usually have at home can save you a lot of time. The fastest shopping trip is one you don't have to take in the first place. Regular pantry cleaning and organisation will save you a lot of time in the long run.

2. **ORGANISE YOUR FRIDGE AND FREEZER.**

   I'm not against having jars of things in the fridge for years (if it's still good, no need to throw it out), but the biggest problem is not knowing what's there. Label things in the freezer (with dates) and make sure you know what's in all those jars lurking in your fridge.

3. **PREP AFTER SHOPPING.**

   Separating prep from cooking is one of the easiest things you can do to speed up your cooking. Try washing and cutting vegetables for the next few days, or cutting or marinating meats, as soon as you get home from shopping. You'll be surprised how much time this can save.

4. **CONVENIENT ISN'T ALWAYS FAST.**

   Knowing your suppliers should be a cornerstone of your cooking. My regular shops include one supermarket, two Asian grocers, three greengrocers, three butchers and one fishmonger, and I'll usually visit two or three in one trip. Sourcing the right quality and type of ingredients allows me to simplify my cooking and be more efficient.

5. **COOK THE SAME DISHES A FEW TIMES.**

   Familiarity is fast. Looking for new ingredients or learning to cook new dishes will always be time-consuming. If you like the look of a dish, make it three or four times. You'll find the ingredients more easily, the dish will taste better the more familiar you are with it, and you'll cook it faster, too. Maybe try one or two new dishes a month. You don't need to make something for the first time every single time you cook.

CHOPPING

6. THE EARLIER THE BETTER.

Preparing after shopping doesn't always work, but there are plenty of other times you can use to get ahead of your schedule. Chopping ingredients or even cooking dinner can be done in the morning after you've made breakfast and before you wash the chopping board. Even cooking dinner at lunch will save you time.

7. SHARPEN YOUR KNIVES.

People ask me all the time what kind of knives they should buy, but the important thing (no matter what knives you have) is to keep them sharp. There's no point buying expensive knives if you're just going to use them blunt. Buy knives that you can keep sharp. Ceramic water sharpeners are great for home use. Try to run your knives through one a couple of times a month, just for a few seconds. Add in a professional sharpen once in a while, too.

8. SET YOUR CHOPPING BOARD.

I use heavy wooden chopping boards at home because they don't slide around. A thin plastic board will benefit from a damp cloth placed underneath to keep it in place. You can't cut properly – or quickly – if your board is running around the bench.

9. IMPROVE YOUR KNIFE SKILLS.

If you see chefs chopping and wish you could do it like they do, you can. Take a bag of carrots and cut them, focusing on proper cutting technique. There are plenty of resources and videos online that can show you how, and understanding the technique will only take about 20 minutes. With just a bit of practice, you'll be cutting like a pro within a week. Deciding to do it is the most important step.

10. USE PREP TRAYS.

'Isn't that just one more thing to wash?!' you might ask, and yes, it is. But using a tray (or even just a plate) to hold all your chopped ingredients will stop you from trying to cut on an overcrowded chopping board. Washing the tray afterwards won't take more than 5 seconds.

11. CUT VEGETABLES FIRST, MEAT SECOND.

This simple trick will save you a trip to the sink to wash your chopping board. Before you start cutting, spend 30 seconds thinking through the most efficient order to chop your ingredients. You'll find the whole cooking process goes a lot more smoothly.

12. USE A BENCH BIN.

Collect compostable scraps and rubbish in a small benchtop bin, bag or even a large prep bowl. It will keep your bench clean and you won't have to run to the bin every few seconds while you're chopping.

13. ENLIST HELP.

Many of us struggle to ask for help in the kitchen. I know it can sometimes feel like other people get in the way when you're cooking, but learning to ask for help is an important skill. Start by asking someone to do a specific task, like picking herbs. Once you get used to it, you'll realise that many hands do make for light work.

COOKING

14. KEEP YOUR BASICS ON HAND.

Next to my stove, I have a tray with my most frequently used basics. There's olive oil, vegetable oil, salt, pepper, sugar, soy sauce, cooking wine, rice vinegar and potato starch. It saves me from running to the pantry every time I cook.

15. THIS APPLIES TO EQUIPMENT, TOO.

A crock with your most-used utensils next to the stove will save you from having to rummage through drawers looking for something when you need it most.

16. VIRTUAL ASSISTANTS MAKE PERFECT KITCHEN TIMERS.

Timers are necessary in any kitchen, and when setting a timer is as simple as saying, 'Hey, Google, set a timer for pasta for ten minutes,' there's nothing to it. I have one with a screen and can often have three or four timers on the go, all lined up with neat little labels, and I won't have lifted a finger to set them.

17. USE A HIGH-SPEED BLENDER.

A good-quality high-speed blender can save a lot of time you might otherwise spend with a slower jug or stick blender trying to get a smooth sauce, soup or purée. You can usually save any straining as well.

18. GET A SPICE DABBA.

If you cook with spices regularly, a spice dabba is a must. It's a small tin with multiple compartments to hold all your most-used spices. In mine, I have ground cumin, ground coriander, ground turmeric, garam masala, gochugaru (Korean chilli powder), ground cloves and smoked paprika.

19. COOK DOUBLE ... OR TRIPLE.

My general rule is that if something is going to cook for longer than an hour, it's more time-efficient to cook a bigger batch and refrigerate or freeze the excess. You basically end up cooking two or three (or more) meals in the time it takes to cook one.

20. PLAN FOR LEFTOVERS.

I don't mean just cooking extra to eat later. Leftovers are pure gold for saving time in the kitchen. A bit of left-over sauce can form the basis of a gravy in another meal. Some cooked vegetables can be chopped and added to a pasta sauce. Never look down on leftovers – they're the ultimate convenience food.

CLEANING

21. USE A SOAPY SPONGE.

In Australia, research shows that we're split about 50:50 on those who fill the sink and those who use a soapy sponge with running water to wash dishes. I'm definitely in the latter camp. Running water is a more efficient way to wash smaller amounts of dishes.

22. WASH STRAIGHT AWAY.

Washing up straight away stops food from drying on to your boards, trays, appliances or pans, and will save you a lot of soaking and scrubbing time. As soon as the food is out of the pan, I head straight to the sink and give the pan a quick scrub under running water with a heat-resistant brush. It takes seconds.

23. HAVE A SYSTEM FOR CLEANING.

Most people have a system for cooking but overlook how important cleaning is to the process. Know where to stack things in the dishwasher. Know what order to clean things that don't go in the dishwasher. Know where to put things away.

24. CLEAN AS YOU GO.

This is an extraordinarily effective time saver. Washing a prep tray or board doesn't take much more time than putting it in the sink to wash later. You'll also find you use less equipment as the same items will be used again and again. One of the most impressive things I remember about my grandmother's cooking was that, even in the middle of preparing a meal, the kitchen was always clean.

25. LINE BAKING TRAYS WITH BAKING PAPER.

A sheet of baking paper at the bottom of a roasting tray or even in the base of a frying pan can avoid a lot of caked-on residue. You can even rinse and re-use the baking paper.

UNDER 10s

LET'S START … FAST. IF YOU'RE IN NEED OF A QUICK MEAL THAT'S READY IN UNDER 10 MINUTES, YOU'RE HARDLY GOING TO BE REACHING INTO YOUR FRIDGE FOR CUTS FOR SLOW BRAISING. NOR WILL YOU BE AFTER DISHES WITH LOTS OF INGREDIENTS TO CHOP AND PREPARE.

The fastest meals are ones that embody all of the elements in this book, and I'm putting them here at the beginning so that you can see what's possible when you cook smarter in every aspect of making your meal.

These are dishes that use ingredients you probably already have on hand. They don't require a huge amount of chopping. They cook quickly (or often not at all), and they won't leave you with a mountain of washing up at the end.

Most importantly, these dishes show us just how simple a meal can be.

The platonic ideal of a 'meal' is often a table laden with abundant food representing all the major food groups, like some kind of Renaissance still life. But meals come in all shapes and sizes and, like tools, meals can be used for different purposes.

If you think serving a bit of cheese and salad for lunch or dinner is 'cheating', disavow yourself of all such notions before you read any further. Not every meal needs to be in perfect nutritional balance, nor does it need a big hunk of meat in the centre of the table.

Good-quality ingredients, assembled simply and without fuss, isn't cheating. Quite the opposite: it's how food should be. There's no correlation between how difficult a meal is to prepare and how good it tastes, or how full it makes you.

With all these fast meals, the most important thing to remember is to never skimp on quality or care.

Great bread, great cheese, well-tended salad greens, good-quality eggs, some nice plates and a glass of wine will be the difference between a sad, forgettable shadow of a meal hurriedly eaten bent over the kitchen sink and something that is elegant in its simplicity and a joy to revisit again and again.

22	SALAD LYONNAISE
25	TOMATO TARTINE
26	CURRIED EGG FURIKAKE
29	THE ORIGINAL CAESAR SALAD
30	BOMBAY CHEESE TOAST
33	CARBONARA FRIED RICE
34	FISHERMAN'S LUNCH
37	ASSIETTE DE CRUDITÉS
39	DAKOS TOAST
40	BLUE CHEESE AND GREEN APPLE SALAD

SALAD LYONNAISE

SERVES 4

Active time
10 minutes

Cooking time
5 minutes

As the name suggests, this salad is a specialty of Lyon, the birthplace of renowned chef Paul Bocuse and arguably the gourmet capital of France. Good-quality bacon is rendered to lend its flavourful oil to dress a simple salad of green leaves.

4 eggs

3 tablespoons extra-virgin olive oil

200 g (7 oz) good-quality thick-cut bacon or speck, cut into very thick lardons

1 short baguette (approx. 20 cm/ 7¾ in), to serve

25 g (1 oz) butter

½ red onion, finely minced

¼ cup (60 ml/2 fl oz) good-quality red-wine vinegar

1 tablespoon dijon mustard

1 head frisée (curly endive) lettuce, washed, spun dry and torn

salt and black pepper, to season

Bring a saucepan of water to a simmer and crack in the eggs. Poach the eggs for about 4 minutes, then drain and set aside.

While the eggs are poaching, heat a frying pan over medium heat and add the oil and bacon. Fry the bacon for about 5 minutes until browned and the fat is rendered. Remove the bacon from the pan, reserving the fat and oil in the pan.

Cut the baguette in half crossways and split in half lengthways. Drizzle each slice of the bread with a little of the reserved oil in the pan (leaving plenty in the pan for the dressing) and spread with butter. Grill the bread on the cut side until golden.

Add the onion to the oil remaining in the pan and fry for 2–3 minutes until softened, then add the vinegar and mustard and whisk to combine.

Pour the warm dressing over the lettuce and toss to combine. Season with salt and pepper. Divide lettuce between serving plates and scatter with the bacon. Top each with a poached egg and serve with a piece of baguette.

Tip

Poaching eggs is as simple as cracking fresh eggs into simmering water. Don't overthink it or overcomplicate it. Some people add vinegar as it's said to help the eggs set better but I've never noticed any difference whatsoever.

TOMATO TARTINE

SERVES 2

Active time
5 minutes

Cooking time
5 minutes

This is the kind of dish that I look to on a warm Australian summer's evening in January or February, when beautifully ripe, seasonal tomatoes on bread is the perfect way to end the day. Choose good-quality tomatoes and you can't go wrong.

2 thick slices sourdough

1 baby gem lettuce, halved

about ¼ cup (60 ml/2 fl oz) olive oil

3 anchovies, finely chopped

1 tablespoon baby capers

juice and zest of ½ lemon

1 teaspoon red-wine vinegar

pinch of sugar

2 good-quality heirloom tomatoes, sliced

½ cup (about 100 g/3½ oz) mixed cherry tomatoes, sliced

salt and black pepper, to season

Heat a large frying pan over high heat. Drizzle the sourdough and cut side of the lettuce with a little of the oil and fry, with a cooking weight placed on top, until one side of each slice of bread is toasted and the lettuce is slightly blackened. Remove and set aside.

Return the pan to the heat and add the remaining oil. Fry the anchovies and capers for a minute until the anchovies disintegrate and the capers are crisp. Add the lemon juice, vinegar and sugar and gently stir to combine.

Place a slice of sourdough and a lettuce half on each plate. Lay the tomatoes over the toast. Season with salt. Spoon over the dressing, and sprinkle with black pepper and a little grated lemon zest (optional) to serve.

Tip

A tartine is the French term for an open-faced sandwich. You could call it a smørrebrød or doorstop if you like, but I think if there's a nice-sounding French word for what you're making then you may as well use it.

SERVES 2

Active time
5 minutes

Cooking time
5 minutes

2 tablespoons olive oil

2 eggs

1½ cups (280 g/10 oz) cooked rice

finely shredded coriander (cilantro), to serve (optional)

 CURRIED FURIKAKE (MAKES EXTRA)

1 teaspoon cumin seeds

1 teaspoon fennel seeds

1 teaspoon mustard seeds

1 tablespoon ground cumin

1 tablespoon garlic flakes

1 tablespoon onion flakes

1 tablespoon dried parsley flakes

2 teaspoons smoked paprika

1 teaspoon gochugaru (Korean chilli powder)

1 teaspoon chilli flakes

2 tablespoons curry powder

1 teaspoon garam masala

2 teaspoons ground turmeric

1 teaspoon ground black pepper

1 teaspoon toasted sesame seeds

1 teaspoon toasted black sesame seeds

1 teaspoon salt flakes

1 tablespoon vegetable stock powder

Tip

Furikake is a staple in Japan, and you won't find a single Japanese home that doesn't have it in a drawer. If you don't want to make your own version, you can find lots of different varieties at most Asian grocers.

CURRIED EGG FURIKAKE

Furikake is a Japanese rice seasoning that comes in hundreds of different varieties. In Japan, furikake is only used for rice, but thinking laterally it also makes an excellent seasoning for other things like vegetables and salads. It commonly includes ingredients such as seaweed and bonito, but this curried version is an excellent seasoning for eggs.

To make the curried furikake, heat a small frying pan over low–medium heat and toast the cumin seeds, fennel seeds and mustard seeds until fragrant. Remove from the pan and mix with the remaining ingredients. Once cooled, store in an airtight container or zip-lock bag. The furikake will keep in the pantry for a few months.

Return the frying pan to low–medium heat and add the oil. Add about a teaspoon of the furikake to the oil and crack the eggs on top. Scatter a little more of the furikake directly on top of the eggs. Fry for about 5 minutes until the eggs are set. Divide the rice between plates, slide the eggs on top of the rice, and scatter with coriander, if using, to serve.

SERVES 2

Active time
10 minutes

Cooking time
5 minutes

THE ORIGINAL CAESAR SALAD

While many modern versions of caesar salad include ingredients such as anchovies and bacon, the original salad invented in 1924 simply consisted of a seasoned dressing of coddled eggs, oil and citrus juice coating long leaves of cos (romaine) lettuce.

1 garlic clove, halved

¾ cup (180 ml/6 fl oz) olive oil

½ baguette, sliced into 1.5 cm (½ in) slices

salt and black pepper, to season

2 eggs

1 teaspoon dijon mustard

1 teaspoon Worcestershire sauce

juice of 1 lime

1 head cos (romaine) lettuce (or 2 heads baby cos), washed and dried

1 cup (100 g/3½ oz) freshly grated parmesan cheese

Rub the inside of a wide bowl with the cut garlic and add a tablespoon of the oil. Heat a large frying pan over medium heat and add the cut garlic and about half the remaining oil. Fry the baguette slices for about 2 minutes on each side until well browned. Season with salt and pepper.

Bring a small saucepan of water to the boil. Prick a small hole in the base of each egg and boil the eggs for 2 minutes. Crack the eggs into the bowl, scooping the white from the shell, and mix in the mustard, Worcestershire sauce, lime juice and the remaining olive oil. Whisk with a fork to combine.

Cut any large leaves of the lettuce lengthways. Add the lettuce to the bowl, stirring to coat completely in the dressing. Transfer to a serving plate and add the parmesan and fried baguette slices. Season with salt and pepper and serve.

Tip

If you want to add anchovies and bacon to your salad, be my guest. I am by no means a traditionalist, but taking a dish back to its origins is often the easiest way to simplify it.

SERVES 4

Active time
5 minutes

Cooking time
5 minutes

BOMBAY CHEESE TOAST

Around India, casual roadside eateries known as dhabas serve all kinds of dishes and local specialties. This savoury egg toast is inspired by countless similar variations that can be found around the country, and it makes for a perfectly simple dinner.

4 eggs

½ cup (125 ml/4 fl oz) milk

¼ teaspoon ground coriander

¼ teaspoon ground cumin

¼ teaspoon ground turmeric

¼ teaspoon Kashmiri chilli powder

½ cup (60 g/2 oz) grated cheese

¼ cup (15 g/½ oz) roughly chopped coriander (cilantro)

1 large red chilli, finely chopped

1 large green chilli, finely chopped

½ red onion, finely diced

8 cherry tomatoes, quartered

salt and black pepper, to season

4 thick slices white bread

25 g (1 oz) butter, cut into 2 cm (¾ in) cubes

your favourite hot sauce, to serve

Beat the eggs and milk together and stir through the spices and cheese. Combine the coriander, chillies, onion and tomato and stir half through the eggs, reserving the remainder for garnish. Season well with salt and pepper. Dip the bread slices in the egg mixture.

Heat a non-stick frying pan over medium heat and add a little butter. With a slotted spoon, place a dollop of the solids from the egg mixture into the pan and place the soaked bread on top. Cook until the cheese is melted, then flip the bread, add a little more butter and fry until the egg is set. Transfer to a plate, scatter with the fresh coriander and tomato mix, and serve with a little hot sauce.

Tip

Non-stick frying pans are great for making quick cheese toast. I just add a handful of grated cheese directly into the pan and place a slice of bread on top. When the cheese has browned enough to release from the pan, the upper side has already stuck to the bread so it's easy to flip.

CARBONARA FRIED RICE

SERVES 2

Active time
5 minutes

Cooking time
5 minutes

Fried rice is, at its most basic, a combination of egg, oil and rice. Here, the addition of a bit of ham, parmesan and black pepper takes it in an unconventional direction, but truth be told there's very little 'carbonara' about this simple fried rice. I've mainly called it that to annoy the carbonarinieri (Italian food police).

2 tablespoons olive oil

½ cup (80 g/2¾ oz) diced ham

25 g (1 oz) butter

4 eggs, beaten

salt and black pepper, to season

3 cups (555 g/1 lb 4 oz) cooked rice

¼ cup (25 g/1 oz) freshly grated parmesan cheese, plus extra to serve

Heat a large non-stick frying pan over medium heat and add the oil and the ham. Fry the ham until it just starts to brown, then add the butter and allow it to melt. Add the egg and, as it cooks, push the edge of the egg in a few times towards the centre of the pan. Season with a little salt and when the eggs are nearly set, add the rice, season very well with salt and mix well. Fry for a few minutes until the rice is lightly toasted, then scatter in the parmesan and mix. Grind over plenty of black pepper and scatter with extra parmesan to serve.

Tip

If you want to add some greenery, a handful of frozen peas or some finely sliced spring onion (scallion) would be excellent choices.

FISHERMAN'S LUNCH

SERVES 2–4

Active time
10 minutes

Cooking time
5 minutes

If a ploughman's lunch is an assembled selection of ham, cheese and pickles, the fisherman's version is arguably even simpler. Spanish conservas are high-quality tinned seafoods, best enjoyed simply and without fuss, and there are a huge variety available. Pair with some tasty, complementary accompaniments for a wonderful meal.

a few thick slices good-quality sourdough

120 g (4½ oz) good-quality tinned Spanish mackerel (or other tinned fish, see Tip, below)

100 g (3½ oz) smoked salmon slices

¼ cup (45 g/1½ oz) cornichons

¼ cup (50 g/1¾ oz) pickled onions

25 g (1 oz) good-quality butter

75 g (2¾ oz) good-quality blue cheese

1 avocado, cut into thick wedges

1 green apple, thinly sliced, to serve

1 lemon, cut into wedges, to serve

SOUR CREAM AND DILL SAUCE

2 tablespoons good-quality mayonnaise

1 teaspoon dijon mustard

100 ml (3½ fl oz) sour cream or crème fraîche

¼ cup (15 g/½ oz) finely shredded dill

salt and pepper, to season

Heat a chargrill pan over high heat and lightly toast the bread. To make the sour cream and dill sauce, combine the ingredients and season well with salt and pepper.

Arrange the tinned fish, smoked salmon, cornichons, pickled onions, butter, blue cheese, avocado, apple and lemon on a plate and serve with the sourdough and the sour cream and dill sauce.

Tip

Good-quality tinned seafood, from unique local stuff to cult artisan brands, is everywhere these days if you keep your eye out. When I'm abroad, I like to stock up on different varieties to bring home as gifts.

ASSIETTE DE CRUDITÉS

SERVES 4

Active time
10 minutes

Cooking time
8 minutes

This literally translates to 'plate of raw vegetables' but I think we can all agree that saying it in French gives it a little bit more sophistication – I'm not even kidding. We tend to look down at things like this, thinking it's a cop-out or cheat dinner, but really it's been a favourite, elegant dish in French dining for ages.

150 g (5½ oz) green beans

1 bunch (approx. 200 g/7 oz) asparagus, trimmed

4 eggs

4 ripe heirloom tomatoes, sliced

salt and black pepper, to season

1 yellow capsicum (bell pepper), thinly sliced

4 radishes, thinly sliced on a mandoline

60 g (2 oz) baby rocket (arugula), washed and trimmed

1 Lebanese (short) cucumber, quartered lengthways

2 carrots, grated

4 pieces cooked beetroot (beet; see Tips, below)

8 anchovies (optional)

baguette, to serve

good-quality whole-egg mayonnaise, to serve

BASIC VINAIGRETTE

1 teaspoon dijon mustard

2 tablespoons white-wine vinegar

juice of ½ lemon

⅓ cup (80 ml/2½ fl oz) extra-virgin olive oil or grapeseed oil

Bring a saucepan of water to the boil. Add the beans and asparagus and cook for just 30 seconds. Remove from the water and set aside. Prick a hole in the base of each egg. Boil the eggs for 8 minutes, refresh in iced water, then peel.

Season the tomatoes well with salt and set aside for 5 minutes.

To make the vinaigrette, combine the mustard, vinegar and lemon juice in a large bowl and slowly whisk in the oil.

Cut the eggs in half. Arrange all the ingredients in piles on a serving plate. Dress with the vinaigrette and serve with toasted baguette and a little mayonnaise.

Tips

Double, triple or even quadruple the vinaigrette recipe and keep it in the fridge. It will keep for about two weeks.

Cooked beetroot is available vacuum sealed from large supermarkets.

SERVES 4

Active time
5 minutes

Cooking time
5 minutes

DAKOS TOAST

Dakos (also known as koukouvagia) is a Greek meze from the island of Crete. Traditionally, dakos is made by topping a dried barley rusk that's been soaked in water with some tomato and mizithra cheese. This simple version doesn't require a passport and is ready in minutes.

1 large wholemeal cob loaf
½ cup (125 ml/4 fl oz) olive oil
4 ripe tomatoes
salt, to season
200 g (7 oz) Greek feta
1 teaspoon dried Greek oregano
1 tablespoon baby capers
¼ cup (40 g/1½ oz) pitted kalamata olives

Heat a chargrill pan over high heat. Cut the cob loaf in half horizontally and drizzle with ⅓ cup (80 ml/2½ fl oz) of the olive oil. Grill the bread, cut side down, until toasted.

Grate the tomatoes into a sieve set over a bowl and season with salt. Place the bread on a serving plate. Use a few spoons of the tomato water to moisten the bread, drizzle with 1 tablespoon of olive oil and spoon the tomatoes over the top. Drizzle with the remaining olive oil, then crumble the feta on top and scatter with oregano, capers and olives.

Tip

You can also bake the loaf in the oven at 150°C (300°F) fan-forced for 30 minutes to dry out the bread if you want to re-create the texture of a Cretan rusk.

SERVES 4

Active time
5 minutes

BLUE CHEESE AND GREEN APPLE SALAD

One of the best dishes I had on my most recent trip to France comprised just two things – a slice of excellent cheese (Langres, if I recall correctly) with a lightly dressed mâche salad, and it made me question why we bother putting cheese plates together at all. Here, the sweet tartness of green apple is an excellent foil for the pungent blue cheese.

1 teaspoon dijon mustard

2 tablespoons apple-cider vinegar

3 tablespoons extra-virgin olive oil

salt and black pepper, to season

120 g (4½ oz) green salad leaves (green oak lettuce and butter lettuce preferred)

1 green apple

100 g (3½ oz) good-quality blue cheese

sourdough baguette, to serve

Combine the mustard, vinegar, oil and a good sprinkle of salt and black pepper to create a simple vinaigrette.

Prepare the salad leaves carefully by trimming any brown parts or thick stems. Wash the greens and spin dry. Thinly slice the apple, preferably on a mandoline, and combine with the leaves and dressing.

Serve the salad with the blue cheese and a hunk of baguette.

Tip

Of course, you can use any cheese you like. I love making this to try out a new cheese as it really puts the cheese front and centre.

LESS TIME SHOPPING

THERE'S A SAYING IN CHINESE CUISINE THAT HALF THE CREDIT FOR A MEAL SHOULD GO TO THE PERSON WHO COLLECTED THE INGREDIENTS. WE TEND TO THINK OF COOKING AS WHAT HAPPENS IN THE KITCHEN, BUT THE PROCESS BEGINS LONG BEFORE THAT.

How long is your average trip to the shops? Once you add up the driving time to get there, car parking, roaming the aisles, shopping, paying, packing, driving back home again and unpacking? Not many of us would get change out of an hour, and it can take much longer.

In this chapter we're talking about recipes that avoid that hassle almost entirely.

Pantry staples aren't just things in your pantry. These days we also need to include things that we might have in our fridges or freezers. The ingredients we choose as our staples are so chosen because they are excellent quality when tinned, dried or frozen. Sometimes even better quality – or at least more suited to cooking – than their fresh counterparts.

You can pod fresh peas in season if you want to, but frozen peas are an absolutely wonderful ingredient: full of nutrients, natural, delicious and convenient. Dried or tinned beans are excellent, too.

Dried pasta is so convenient I've devoted an entire chapter to it a little later in the book – and dried rice is just as useful.

Pickles like kimchi keep for an age in the fridge, so they're something you can always have on hand, and I'd be a little surprised if most of us didn't have a potato or carrot sitting in the fridge or pantry right now. Ditto for onion, garlic or ginger, and if you know how to combine these ingredients together without having to rush out for more then you've immediately saved yourself a big chunk of time.

Eggs, however, might take the prize for me for being the ultimate in natural convenience foods. Their versatility, deliciousness and in-built convenience is the reason they're a staple in just about every cuisine. If you've got eggs in your fridge, you've got a meal at any time of day.

Of course, I don't expect you to have every single ingredient in every one of these recipes at all times, but if you find yourself with a few green beans then maybe Carrot and green bean stew (page 53) might be on the menu. A bit of lettuce and bacon lying around? Add your staples to that and you'll have Little French peas (page 48).

There's no need to follow any of these recipes exactly. They're more ideas to spark creativity than specifics that are set in stone.

46	KIDNEY BEAN CURRY
48	LITTLE FRENCH PEAS
51	KERALA EGG CURRY
53	CARROT AND GREEN BEAN STEW
54	ALOO MATAR WITH BROWN BUTTER TADKA
57	KIMCHI AND GARLIC BUTTER FRIED RICE
59	FROZEN PEA SOUP WITH BACON AND CORN CROUTONS
60	TAMAGO-DON
63	EDAMAME SUCCOTASH
64	RICOTTA EGGS ON TOAST

SERVES 4

Active time
10 minutes

Cooking time
35 minutes

KIDNEY BEAN CURRY
Rajma masala

If you haven't grown up with food from the Indian subcontinent it's easy to get stuck on the idea of curries being meaty, slow-cooked stews that take hours. Most curries – especially vegetarian ones – don't stew for hours at all.

2 tablespoons vegetable oil

1 teaspoon cumin seeds

1 red onion, finely chopped

1 teaspoon salt

3 garlic cloves, grated

2 cm (¾ in) piece fresh ginger, grated

1 small green chilli, sliced

400 g (14 oz) tinned diced tomatoes

1 tablespoon ground coriander

½ teaspoon ground turmeric

2 teaspoons garam masala

2 teaspoons Kashmiri chilli powder

800 g (1 lb 12 oz) tinned red kidney beans, drained

1 tablespoon dried fenugreek leaves (kasuri methi)

¼ cup (15 g/½ oz) roughly chopped coriander (cilantro; optional)

cooked basmati rice, to serve

Heat a saucepan over medium heat and add the oil and cumin, allowing the seeds to crackle. Add the onion and salt and fry for about 5 minutes until lightly golden. Add the garlic, ginger and chilli and fry for a further minute.

Add the tomatoes and cook for about 5 minutes, then add the ground spices and cook for 2–3 minutes until the mixture thickens. Add the beans and about 1–2 cups (250–500 ml/8½–17 fl oz) water. Cover and simmer for 15 minutes, then mash a few of the beans to thicken the mixture and simmer for a further 5 minutes.

Stir through the fenugreek leaves and coriander, if using. Serve with rice.

Tip

Dried fenugreek leaves (kasuri methi) have a delicious flavour and aroma that's similar to celery, but slightly more herbaceous. It's the key flavour in butter chicken, and I keep it on hand in my pantry all the time. It's a convenient dried ingredient for finishing curries in the same way a sprinkling of aromatic fresh herbs might.

SERVES 4

Active time
5 minutes

Cooking time
10–35 minutes

LITTLE FRENCH PEAS
Petits pois à la Française

Many classic cuisines use a little bit of meat (in this case, speck) to add umami to a dish of vegetables. It's an excellent, healthy and efficient way to cook. Don't treat this like a side dish. It's the main event.

200 g (7 oz) speck, cut into thick lardons

2 heads baby cos (romaine) lettuce, halved

4 baby onions, peeled and halved

3 cups (520 g/1 lb 2 oz) frozen baby peas

¼ cup (60 ml/2 fl oz) white wine, water or stock

100 g (3½ oz) butter, cut into cubes

baguette, to serve

Heat a large frying pan over medium heat, add the speck and fry until golden. Remove and set aside. Add the cos and baby onions, cut side down, and fry until well browned and slightly blackened.

Add the peas and wine, and bring to a simmer. Add the butter, cover and simmer over very low heat for 5–25 minutes (see Tip, below) until the onions are tender and the sauce is reduced to a coating consistency. Toss the lardons back through the dish and serve.

This goes wonderfully with a few slices of baguette.

Tip

You can cook this dish for as little as 5 minutes if you want the peas and lettuce to be bright and crisp, but I prefer to cook it for about 25 minutes until the peas have lost a bit of their colour and the lettuce is more wilted. Longer cooking, which is also more traditional, gives the dish a stewed, luxurious character.

KERALA EGG CURRY

SERVES 4

Active time
10 minutes

Cooking time
20 minutes

South Indian dishes are often considered lighter than their northern counterparts, and this egg curry is a staple in Keralan homes.

8 eggs

2 tablespoons coconut oil

½ teaspoon yellow mustard seeds

1 teaspoon fennel seeds

1 sprig curry leaves (optional)

1 large red onion, finely sliced

2 tablespoons garlic and ginger paste (or 3 garlic cloves and 3 cm/1¼ in fresh ginger, grated)

salt, to season

1 large green chilli, sliced

¼ teaspoon ground turmeric

1 tablespoon ground coriander

1 teaspoon ground black pepper

2 teaspoons Kashmiri chilli powder

1 teaspoon garam masala

½ cup (125 ml/4 fl oz) tomato passata (puréed tomatoes)

400 ml (13½ fl oz) coconut milk

cooked rice, paratha or bread, to serve

Bring a pot of water to the boil and boil the eggs for 8 minutes. Peel under running water and set aside.

Heat a frying pan over medium heat and add the oil. Add the mustard and fennel seeds and allow to crackle. Add the curry leaves, if using, onion, garlic and ginger paste, salt and chilli and fry until the onion is lightly browned. Add the ground spices and mix well.

Add the passata and coconut milk and bring to a simmer. Cook for about 10 minutes until the sauce comes together, then add the eggs and stir to coat. Serve with rice, paratha or bread.

Tip

Some recipes call for cutting a few slits in the white of the egg to allow the flavour to penetrate it. Others fry the eggs after boiling to roughen the surface. I've never found either to be necessary, but I thought I'd just let you know.

CARROT AND GREEN BEAN STEW

SERVES 4

Active time
10 minutes

Cooking time
15 minutes

I've called this a stew because in English we don't really have a term for this kind of cooking where vegetables are fried in oil and then gently cooked in their own juices. In North India this process is known as sabzi, but it's also a popular method used across Pakistan, Afghanistan and elsewhere in the region.

½ cup (125 ml/4 fl oz) vegetable oil

200 g (7 oz) green beans, tailed

2 carrots, sliced into thick batons

1 onion, thinly sliced

3 garlic cloves, minced

2 teaspoons ground coriander

1 teaspoon ground turmeric

½ teaspoon Korean or Kashmiri chilli powder

2 tomatoes, diced

salt, to season

½ cup (10 g/¼ oz) mint, torn, to serve

SALTED YOGHURT

1 garlic clove, minced

300 g (10½ oz) thick yoghurt

salt, to season

Heat the oil in a large saucepan over medium–high heat and fry the beans in batches until wrinkled. Remove from the oil and transfer to a bowl. Fry the carrot until browned and add to the bowl with the beans.

Carefully remove a bit of the oil from the pot, leaving about 2–3 tablespoons. Reduce the heat to medium and add the onion and garlic and fry for a minute. Add the coriander, turmeric and chilli powder and mix well.

Return the beans and carrot to the pot. Stir well, then add the tomato and season well with salt. Reduce the heat to very low, then cover and simmer for about 10 minutes.

While the beans are simmering, make the salted yoghurt by mixing the garlic with the yoghurt and seasoning well with salt.

Spread the yoghurt onto a serving plate. Top with the beans and carrot and scatter with the mint to serve.

Tip

I use Korean or Kashmiri chilli powder for its vibrant red colour and strong flavour. Gochugaru (Korean chilli powder) is available in a variety of heat levels and coarseness, which allows you to choose according to your preference.

SERVES 4

Active time
10 minutes

Cooking time
30 minutes

ALOO MATAR WITH BROWN BUTTER TADKA

Potatoes from your pantry and peas from your freezer combine perfectly in this iconic Indian dish, but the best thing about it for me is that every ingredient is something I have in my kitchen at all times.

2 tablespoons vegetable oil

10 g (¼ oz) butter

1 teaspoon cumin seeds

1 small onion, finely chopped

2 garlic cloves, roughly chopped

2 cm (¾ in) piece fresh ginger, roughly chopped

½ cup (125 ml/4 fl oz) tomato passata (puréed tomatoes)

½ teaspoon salt

1 teaspoon vegetable stock powder

½ teaspoon ground cumin

1 teaspoon ground coriander

½ teaspoon Korean or Kashmiri chilli powder

¼ teaspoon ground turmeric

1 teaspoon garam masala

2 large potatoes, cut into 1.5 cm (½ in) cubes

1 cup (155 g/5½ oz) frozen peas

1 tablespoon dried fenugreek leaves (kasuri methi; optional)

TADKA

20 g (¾ oz) unsalted butter

½ teaspoon cumin seeds

1 garlic clove, sliced

¼ teaspoon Korean or Kashmiri chilli powder

Heat a large, lidded frying pan over medium heat. Add the oil, butter and cumin. When the cumin seeds start to crackle, add the onion, garlic and ginger and fry for about 3 minutes until softened. Add the passata and cook for a minute or two, then add the salt, stock powder and ground spices. Stir to combine, then add the potato and peas and about ½ cup (125 ml/4 fl oz) water. You can add more water if it's too dry, but you don't want it to be too soupy. Cover and cook for 20 minutes until the potatoes are tender, then stir through the fenugreek leaves. Transfer to a serving plate.

To make the tadka, heat the butter, cumin and garlic in a small saucepan over medium heat until the butter and garlic are browned. Add the chilli powder and immediately pour over the vegetables, then serve.

Tip

The tadka or tempering process refers to frying aromatic spices in a little oil (or, in this case, butter) either at the beginning or end of cooking to add an additional level of flavour. Don't skip it.

SERVES 2

Active time
5 minutes

Cooking time
10 minutes

KIMCHI AND GARLIC BUTTER FRIED RICE

All fried rice dishes rely on the combination of egg and rice. In this dish, the egg is added on top when serving rather than fried with the rice. The added 'sprinkles' of sesame seeds, spring onions (scallions) and nori are unmissable highlights.

1 tablespoon vegetable oil, plus extra for frying the eggs

2 eggs

4 garlic cloves, sliced

1 cup (150 g/5½ oz) kimchi, roughly chopped

1 teaspoon sesame oil

1 tablespoon gochujang (Korean fermented chilli paste)

3 cups (555 g/1 lb 4 oz) cooked koshihikari (sushi) rice, refrigerated

salt, to season

20 g (¾ oz) butter

1 tablespoon toasted sesame seeds

2 tablespoons finely chopped spring onions (scallions)

black pepper

1 pack Korean toasted seasoned nori, to serve

Heat a large frying pan over medium heat, add the oil and fry the eggs until the white is set but the yolks are still runny. Remove from the pan and set aside. Return the pan to the heat, add the garlic and fry until fragrant and lightly browned. Add the kimchi, sesame oil and gochujang and fry until fragrant. Add the rice and season very well with salt. Fry for about 3 minutes until the rice is well mixed and starting to toast. Stir through the butter.

Divide the rice between two bowls and top each with a fried egg. Scatter with sesame seeds, spring onion and plenty of black pepper. Serve with the nori.

Tip

My wife, Asami, always asks why my fried kimchi dishes taste so good and, without wanting to detract from the perfect balance of savoury and sour in good kimchi, the secret is butter. Kimchi and butter are a match made in heaven.

SERVES 4

Active time
10 minutes

Cooking time
10 minutes

FROZEN PEA SOUP WITH BACON AND CORN CROUTONS

Frozen vegetables are generally excellent, but peas and corn kernels are particularly good choices. They're cheap, nutritious, save you plenty of labour and they taste great, too. You could of course use frozen spinach here instead of fresh – it's another vegetable that freezes extremely well.

1 tablespoon olive oil, plus extra to serve

1 onion, roughly chopped

4 cups (1 litre/34 fl oz) vegetable stock

1 kg (2 lb 3 oz) frozen peas

60 g (2 oz) baby spinach

salt and black pepper, to season

BACON AND CORN CROUTONS

2 tablespoons olive oil

2 rashers bacon, roughly chopped

2 slices white bread, cut into 1 cm (½ in) cubes

1 cup (150 g/5½ oz) frozen corn kernels

Heat a large saucepan over medium heat and add the oil and onion. Fry for about 3 minutes until the onion is lightly browned, then add the stock and bring to a simmer. Add the peas and spinach and return to a simmer. Once the soup starts to simmer again, remove from the heat and blend the soup until smooth. Season with salt and pepper.

To make the bacon and corn croutons, heat a frying pan over medium heat and add the oil and bacon. Fry until the bacon is crisp, then add the bread and corn and fry until the bread is browned. Top the soup with the croutons and a drizzle of olive oil.

Tip

To blend hot ingredients, remove the plug from the top of the blender, cover it with a tea towel instead and start the blender slowly. This will allow steam to escape so pressure doesn't build up in the jug and cause an accident.

SERVES 1

Active time
10 minutes

Cooking time
10 minutes

TAMAGO-DON

A donburi or don in Japan refers to a rice bowl, often topped with any number of ingredients, such as fried pork cutlets (katsu-don), tempura (ten-don) or thinly sliced stewed beef (gyu-don). This egg version (tamago-don) is about as simple as it gets, and it's all made from ingredients you probably have in your pantry.

2 dried shiitake mushrooms

1 tablespoon soy sauce, plus a little extra to serve

1 tablespoon mirin

½ teaspoon sugar

½ small onion, sliced

2 eggs, beaten

1½ cups (280 g/10 oz) cooked koshihikari (sushi) rice

1 spring onion (scallion), finely sliced

Japanese seven spice (shichimi), to serve (optional)

Cover the mushrooms with 1½ cups (375 ml/12½ fl oz) boiling water and stand for 15 minutes until softened. Remove the mushrooms from the liquid, reserving the liquid, cut off the stalks and thinly slice the caps.

Place the mushroom soaking liquid in a small frying pan over medium–high heat and add the soy sauce, mirin, sugar, onion and sliced mushrooms. Bring to a simmer and cook for about 3 minutes or until the onion is softened. Pour the egg into the liquid in the pan and stir once or twice. Simmer until the egg is just set, then slide the egg mixture out of the pan and onto a bowl of rice. Scatter with spring onion, drizzle over a little extra soy sauce and serve with a little Japanese seven spice, if using.

Tip

Mirin is a sweet Japanese cooking wine used to add sweetness and gloss to dishes. It's a staple seasoning in my kitchen and if you cook a lot of East Asian food it should be a staple in yours, too.

SERVES 4

Active time
10 minutes

Cooking time
15 minutes

EDAMAME SUCCOTASH

North American succotash originated from Native American cuisines and, at its most basic, combines the nutritional balance of cooking a grain (in this case, corn) together with a legume (I've used edamame here). It's most commonly made with broad beans, but you can use any beans you like.

3 tablespoons olive oil

150 g (5½ oz) bacon or speck (in a block), cut into thick lardons

1 small onion, minced

2 garlic cloves, minced

1 red capsicum (bell pepper), finely diced

2 cups (310 g/11 oz) frozen edamame

2 cups (400 g/14 oz) frozen corn kernels

1 teaspoon smoked paprika

salt and black pepper, to season

200 g (7 oz) cherry tomatoes, halved

25 g (1 oz) butter

1 teaspoon apple-cider vinegar

¼ cup (15 g/½ oz) roughly chopped basil

¼ cup (15 g/½ oz) roughly chopped parsley

Heat a large frying pan over medium heat and add the oil and bacon. Fry the bacon until crisp, then remove from the pan. Add the onion and garlic and fry for about 4 minutes until softened. Add the capsicum and cook for about 2 minutes. Add the edamame, corn and paprika and season well with salt and pepper. Cook for about 5 minutes then return the bacon to the pan with the cherry tomatoes and butter, toss together and cook for about a minute just to melt the butter and soften the tomatoes. Stir through the vinegar, basil and parsley to serve.

Tip

If you don't have fresh herbs on hand for this dish, you can also use dried. Add them a little earlier in the cooking process so that they can release more of their flavour. If you don't have the dried herbs either, just leave them out.

RICOTTA EGGS ON TOAST

SERVES 4

Active time
5 minutes

Cooking time
5 minutes

If eggs on toast seems too 'breakfast-y' to you, that's just because dishes like these are made so that you don't have to run to the shops before cooking them. What's convenient for breakfast will be convenient for dinner, too, and a dish this luxurious is probably more suited to an evening meal than first thing in the morning.

1 large thick slice sourdough
2 tablespoons olive oil
20 g (¾ oz) butter
3 eggs, beaten
100 g (3½ oz) ricotta
salt and pepper, to season
1 tablespoon finely chopped chives
freshly grated pecorino, to serve

Heat a chargrill pan over high heat. Drizzle the bread with the oil and grill until toasted to your liking.

Heat a small frying pan over medium heat and add the butter. Pour in the egg and mix with a spatula until starting to set. Add the ricotta and mix with the eggs until the eggs are softly set. Season well with salt and transfer on to the toast. Scatter with the chives, grind over a little black pepper and grate over the pecorino.

Tip

I prefer to cook bread by grilling or frying it in contact with a pan rather than trying to toast it. The direct conducted heat of contact gives you a crisp exterior without drying out the interior like convected or radiated heat can.

LESS TIME CHOPPING

OTHER THAN SHOPPING, USUALLY THE MOST LABOUR-INTENSIVE PART OF COOKING IS THE PREPARATION, AND BY THIS I MEAN THE TIME SPENT STANDING AT A BENCH SLICING, DICING AND CHOPPING INGREDIENTS.

Sometimes when my wife, Asami, is cooking something that involves a lot of chopping, she'll ask me to do that part before she takes care of the rest, knowing that I'll be faster than she is.

Let me give you the hard truth first: if chopping takes you a long time while cooking, the best way to reduce this time is to learn how to chop faster.

Knife skills are important in the kitchen. Even though many of us cook our whole lives, our knife skills don't improve all that much. We find our groove and we stick to it. It's comfortable, and each night when we cook our goal isn't really to improve our cooking. We're just trying to get food on the table.

I cooked for years without ever bothering to learn the 'cheffy' cutting that the professionals do. There didn't seem to be much point. Chefs do things the proper way, but we home cooks just get through with what works.

It was only when I started working in a kitchen that I understood the value of it. When you're just cutting one onion or carrot, you can get away with doing it any way you want. But cut 10 kilograms of onions or carrots and you're going to want to find the most efficient way to do it.

The thing I realised was that even if you're not cutting large volumes, these small efficiencies – like cutting a vegetable a little faster than you might otherwise have – can have a huge impact. Not only that, your food will taste better, too. Knife skills allow us to create the texture of our food, and texture is so important to good food.

When I finally decided to learn how to cut properly, it honestly took half an hour to understand the basics and then a few meals of slow cutting to reach the point where I was already cutting faster and more than I used to.

I'm not going to try to teach you how to cut properly here. There are plenty of online resources and videos that can do that far better than a book can.

Just making the decision to learn to cut properly is the important part. After you understand the theory, every meal you make becomes practice.

No matter how good your knife skills get, chopping will always be a large part of the time you spend cooking. In this chapter we're looking at meals that reduce the amount of cutting you need to do. If it's the tedious part of cooking for you, take careful note.

In this chapter, we'll use pre-chopped frozen vegetables, and cuts like drumsticks and mince that don't need to be chopped at all. Sausages are a favourite of mine for quick preparation, because not only are they pre-cut, they're pre-seasoned as well.

I've also included a couple of steaks for sharing that can be cooked before being sliced – cutting cooked food is always easier than raw.

71	FROZEN VEGETABLE FRIED RICE
73	ROAST PUMPKIN WITH TAHINI SAUCE
74	RUMP CAP WITH QUICK CHIMICHURRI
77	TURKISH TANDOORI DRUMSTICKS
78	BEEF TAGLIATA
80	SWEDISH MINCE
83	SAUSAGES IN CIDER AND MUSTARD
85	TWICE-ROASTED POTATOES
86	CHEESEBURGER SANG CHOY BAO
88	GARLIC CHICKEN DRUMSTICKS
91	LAMB KHEEMA

FROZEN VEGETABLE FRIED RICE

SERVES 5

Active time
10 minutes

Cooking time
15 minutes

Frozen diced vegetables are a life-saver for quick fried rice – no chopping required and they're the perfect size. I add lap cheong (Chinese sausage) and prawns (shrimp) to mine too as they are two ingredients I always have in the freezer.

½ cup (125 ml/4 fl oz) vegetable oil

1 small onion, finely diced

4 garlic cloves, minced

2 lap cheong (Chinese sausages), sliced (optional)

1½ cups (170 g/6 oz) mixed diced frozen vegetables

100 g (3½ oz) frozen prawns (shrimp), thawed (optional)

salt and white pepper, to season

1 teaspoon chicken stock powder

4 cups (740 g/1 lb 10 oz) cooked rice

3 eggs, beaten

Heat a large frying pan over medium heat and add 2 tablespoons of the oil. Add the onion and garlic and fry for about 2 minutes until starting to brown. Add the lap cheong, if using, and fry for a few minutes until the sausage is starting to brown. Add the vegetables and prawns, if using, and cook until the vegetables are thawed and the prawns lightly cooked. Season with salt, pepper and stock powder.

Add the rice to the pan and press with the back of a spatula to break it up. Season well with salt. Move the contents of the pan to one side and add the egg to the clear side. Mix the egg vigorously until cooked and starting to break into small pieces. Mix with the rice. Season to taste and serve.

Tip

If cutting onions makes you cry, a sharp knife and good cutting technique will help. A sharp knife doesn't bruise the onion as you cut, and good cutting technique finishes the job quickly while keeping your back straight and your eyes and nose away from your chopping board.

SERVES 4

Active time
5 minutes

Cooking time
45 minutes

ROAST PUMPKIN WITH TAHINI SAUCE

Cutting pumpkin can be a pain, and perhaps even a dangerous proposition if you don't have a big, sharp knife. My solution is not to cut it at all. I buy half butternut pumpkins and roast them as is. You don't even need to scrape out the seeds before you roast it!

½ butternut pumpkin

1 red onion, quartered

3 tablespoons olive oil

salt and black pepper, to season

½ cup (135 g/5 oz) tahini

juice of ½ lemon

¼ cup (5 g/⅛ oz) mint, torn or roughly chopped

1 handful of roasted almonds, roughly chopped

lemon wedges, to serve

grilled sourdough, to serve

Heat your oven to 220°C (430°F) fan-forced and line a roasting tin with baking paper. Place the pumpkin and onion in the prepared tin, drizzle with a little of the oil, season with salt and pepper and roast for 45 minutes.

Combine the tahini, lemon juice and about ½ cup (125 ml/4 fl oz) water and mix to a smooth sauce. Season with salt.

Scoop the seeds out of the pumpkin and discard. Drizzle over the tahini sauce and remaining oil, and scatter with the mint and almonds. Season well with salt and pepper and serve with lemon wedges and grilled sourdough.

Tip

Don't stress too much about chopping herbs. Rough is best, and if you wanted to put the knife away completely you can just tear them, or even leave them whole.

SERVES 4

Active time
10 minutes

Cooking time
15 minutes

Resting time
1 hour 10 minutes

RUMP CAP WITH QUICK CHIMICHURRI

Rump cap (picanha) is a fantastic cut of meat that is still relatively affordable here in Australia. It's a favourite in South America for its rich fat cap and meaty flavour. Cut it into steaks, or even roast it whole (at 180°C/360°F for about 30 minutes). If you don't want to eat the full rump cap, it's an affordable cut for buying whole and dividing into thick steaks for refrigerating or freezing.

1 beef rump cap (picanha), about 1.5 kg (3 lb 5 oz)

salt and pepper, to season

approx. ¼ cup (60 ml/2 fl oz) vegetable oil

 QUICK CHIMICHURRI

2 garlic cloves, grated on a microplane

3 thin spring onions (scallions), finely sliced

1 teaspoon chilli flakes

¼ teaspoon ground black pepper

½ cup (125 ml/4 fl oz) good-quality olive oil

¼ cup (60 ml/2 fl oz) red-wine vinegar

1 cup (60 g/2 oz) loosely packed parsley, finely chopped

1 teaspoon dried oregano

sugar and salt, to season

To make the chimichurri, stir all the ingredients together and set aside for at least 1 hour before using.

To cook the rump cap, first score the fat cap in a cross-hatch pattern. Cut the rump cap into 6 cm (2½ in) thick steaks and season well with salt and pepper. Drizzle the steaks all over with oil.

Heat your barbecue hotplate, grill or a frying pan over medium heat until very hot. Sear the steaks on each side until well browned and sear the fat cap to render some of the fat. Flip the steaks until they reach an internal temperature of 50°C (120°F) when tested with a meat thermometer, then remove from the heat and rest for about 10 minutes before cutting into thick slices.

Serve the sliced rump cap topped with the chimichurri.

Tip

The chimichurri takes a bit of chopping, but it will keep in the fridge for about a week. You can also make it in a small food processor if you prefer. Just don't cut it too finely. It shouldn't be a purée.

TURKISH TANDOORI DRUMSTICKS

SERVES 4–6

Active time
5 minutes

Cooking time
45 minutes

Resting time
overnight (optional)

Red pepper paste (biber salçasi) is a staple in Turkish households. It's great as a marinade ingredient with these drumsticks, but I also add it to stews, pasta sauces or anywhere else I would normally use tomato paste.

8 chicken drumsticks

¼ cup (60 ml/2 fl oz) olive oil

¼ cup (60 g/2 oz) Turkish hot red pepper paste (biber salçasi), or tomato paste (concentrated purée)

¼ cup (60 g/2 oz) thick yoghurt, plus extra to serve

3 garlic cloves, grated

2 teaspoons ground cumin

2 teaspoons sumac, plus extra to serve

1 teaspoon Kashmiri chilli powder

1 teaspoon salt

sliced red onion, to serve

toasted pitas, to serve

roughly chopped flat-leaf (Italian) parsley, to serve

Combine the drumsticks with all the ingredients except the onion. Refrigerate overnight or even for a few days if you can, but if you can't, you can just cook them straight away.

Heat your oven to 200°C (390°F) fan-forced. Place a piece of baking paper in the base of a roasting tin and arrange the drumsticks on top. Roast for 45 minutes.

Spread a little extra yoghurt on a serving plate and arrange the drumsticks on top. Serve with the red onion sprinkled with a little extra sumac, toasted pitas and parsley.

Tip

These can also be made on a low barbecue. If barbecuing, cut thick slits into the drumsticks all the way to the bone so they cook more quickly.

SERVES 4

Active time
10 minutes

Cooking time
15 minutes

Resting time
5 minutes

BEEF TAGLIATA

The only thing that needs to be cut in this recipe for 'sliced beef' is the beef itself, and even that is done after cooking. Meat tightens during the cooking process, and it's much easier to cut afterwards.

½ cup (125 ml/4 fl oz) olive oil

1 garlic clove, bruised

2 rosemary sprigs

zest and juice of ½ small lemon, plus wedges to serve

1 sirloin steak, about 5 cm/2 in thick (around 600 g/1 lb 5 oz)

salt and pepper, to season

60 g (2 oz) rocket (arugula)

good-quality parmesan cheese (in a block, for shaving), to serve

Heat a frying pan over medium heat and add about 2 teaspoons of the oil. Fry the garlic, rosemary and lemon zest for about 30 seconds until fragrant, then transfer to a bowl and pour over the remaining oil. If you can let this stand to infuse for about 10 minutes it will be more fragrant, but don't worry if you can't.

Season the steak well with salt and pepper and fry until well browned but just rare. Remove the steak from the pan, drizzle with the infused oil and rest for 5 minutes.

Toss the rocket with some more of the oil and the lemon juice. Shave plenty of parmesan into the rocket with a vegetable peeler and toss to combine. Season with black pepper.

Slice the steak and place on a serving plate with the rocket salad. Drizzle with extra oil and season with more salt and pepper.

Tip

A sharp knife is essential for cutting meat. Rolling wheel sharpeners are great for home use if a sharpening stone is too intimidating. Otherwise, look at getting your knives professionally sharpened every few months.

SERVES 4

Active time
10 minutes

Cooking time
25 minutes

SWEDISH MINCE

Why go to the effort of making Swedish meatballs when this delicious savoury mince requires no cutting or rolling? To simplify it even further, you could serve with buttered new potatoes (see page 83) instead of mashed potato.

2 tablespoons vegetable oil

500 g (1 lb 2 oz) mixed minced (ground) beef and pork

2 onions, roughly chopped

3 tablespoons plain (all-purpose) flour

1 cup (250 ml/8½ fl oz) beef stock

1 tablespoon dark soy sauce

1 tablespoon Worcestershire sauce

¼ teaspoon ground nutmeg

¼ teaspoon allspice

150 ml (5 fl oz) thickened (whipping) cream

shredded dill, to serve

dill pickles, to serve

lingonberry jam or cranberry sauce, to serve

MASHED POTATO

1 kg (2 lb 3 oz) potatoes, peeled and cut into large chunks

50 g (1¾ oz) butter

100 ml (3½ fl oz) milk, warmed

Heat a deep, lidded frying pan over medium heat and add the oil. Form the mince into a giant patty and fry on each side until well browned. Add the onions after one side of the meat has browned. When the onions have browned, break up the mince, add the flour and mix well. Add the stock, soy sauce, Worcestershire, nutmeg and allspice, stir, then cover and simmer for 15 minutes. Stir through the cream.

To make the mashed potato, place the potato in a large saucepan of water and bring to a boil. Cook for 20 minutes or until the potato is tender, then drain and mash with the butter and milk until smooth.

Divide the mince mixture and mashed potato between plates. Sprinkle with dill and serve with pickles and lingonberry jam or cranberry sauce.

Tip

Making the mince into a big patty is a great technique to use because your mince will brown before it starts releasing its juices and cooling down the pan. Just break up the patty after it browns.

SERVES 4

Active time
10 minutes

Cooking time
45 minutes

SAUSAGES IN CIDER AND MUSTARD

A butcher friend once told me that the best advice he ever received on running his shop was to put his best efforts into his mince and sausages, because those are what keep customers coming back. It's true. When you find a butcher with good mince and sausages, stick with them.

20 g (¾ oz) butter

8 good-quality pork sausages

2 onions, thickly sliced

2 tablespoons plain (all-purpose) flour

5 thyme sprigs

½ teaspoon salt

1½ cups (375 ml/12½ fl oz) dry apple cider

1–2 tablespoons wholegrain mustard

2 green apples, peeled, cored and cut into wedges

100 ml (3½ fl oz) sour cream

black pepper, to season

BUTTERED NEW POTATOES

1 kg (2 lb 3 oz) potatoes, peeled and cut into large chunks

2 tablespoons salt, plus extra to season

50 g (1¾ oz) butter

Heat a large, lidded low casserole dish over medium heat and add the butter. Add the sausages and onion and fry for about 10 minutes until well-browned. Stir in the flour, then add the thyme, salt, apple cider, mustard and apple. Stir well, cover and simmer for 20 minutes. Stir through the sour cream and season with black pepper.

To make the buttered new potatoes, place the potato in a large pot and cover with cold water. Add the salt and bring to a simmer. Cook for about 15 minutes until the potato is tender or until a small, sharp knife can be inserted into the centre and withdrawn easily. Drain well.

Heat a large frying pan over medium heat and add the potato and butter. Fry until lightly browned. Season well with salt. Serve with the sausages.

Tip

You can try different versions of this based on what you have to hand. Switch the pork sausages for beef, replace the apples with extra onions and switch out the cider for beer or red wine and you've got a completely different dish.

TWICE-ROASTED POTATOES

SERVES 2

Active time
5 minutes

Cooking time
2 hours

This is the easiest way to make crispy roast potatoes. I put the potatoes in the oven on a timer in the morning to roast for an hour and then just go about my day. After roasting, the potatoes just stay in the oven all day. When I come home I cut them and roast them a second time and they're done. Foolproof.

1 kg (2 lb 3 oz) potatoes, scrubbed but unpeeled

½ cup (125 ml/4 fl oz) vegetable oil

salt, to season

HERB RANCH

½ cup (125 g/4½ oz) mayonnaise

½ cup (125 g/4½ oz) sour cream

2 teaspoons apple-cider vinegar

½ teaspoon garlic powder

1 teaspoon onion powder

1 teaspoon mustard powder

½ teaspoon dried parsley

½ teaspoon dried dill

½ teaspoon dried chives

½ teaspoon dried tarragon

salt and black pepper, to season

To make the herb ranch, combine the ingredients in a bowl.

Heat your oven to 200°C (390°F) fan-forced. Place the potatoes in a roasting tin and roast for 1 hour. Remove from the oven and allow to cool to room temperature. At this stage, you can refrigerate the potatoes if you won't need them for a day or two.

Heat your oven again to 200°C (390°F) fan-forced. Cut the potatoes into large chunks (around six pieces per potato) and squash each piece gently with your hand. Return the potatoes to the roasting tray and pour the oil over the top. Stir to coat in the oil and roast for another hour, stirring the potatoes halfway through cooking. Scatter with plenty of salt and serve with the ranch.

Tip

You can roast these potatoes ahead of time and freeze them (even after cutting and crushing). They'll then be on hand, ready to cook for the second time, whenever you need them. It's like making your own oven fries.

SERVES 4

Active time
10 minutes

Cooking time
25 minutes

CHEESEBURGER SANG CHOY BAO

Sang choy bao means 'lettuce parcel' and this easy one-pot mince is great wrapped in a single or double layer of lettuce. You could easily use burger buns instead of lettuce though (or as well as), or turn this into a simple pasta casserole (see Tip, below).

3 tablespoons olive oil

500 g (1 lb 2 oz) minced (ground) beef

1 large onion, diced

2 cups (120 g/4½ oz) mixed frozen vegetables

1 tablespoon dark soy sauce

¼ cup (60 g/2 oz) American mustard, plus extra to serve

¼ cup (60 g/2 oz) tomato sauce, plus extra to serve

salt and pepper, to season

2 cups (250 g/9 oz) shredded tasty cheese

1 head iceberg lettuce, separated into cups

1 red onion, sliced, to serve

1 tomato, sliced, to serve

dill pickles, to serve

Heat a shallow casserole pan over high heat and add the oil. Mould the mince into a large patty and fry on both sides until well browned. Add the onion and fry for about 2 minutes until the onion is softened and lightly browned, then break up the patty and add the vegetables, soy sauce, mustard and tomato sauce. Season well with salt and pepper. Add a little water if needed, and cook for about 3 minutes until the mince is cooked through. Scatter with the cheese and grill under an overhead oven grill (broiler) for 10 minutes until the cheese is melted and bubbling.

Serve with the lettuce cups, red onion, tomato, pickles and extra mustard and tomato sauce so people can roll up their own.

Tip

To turn this into a one-pot pasta cheeseburger casserole instead, you can add 2 cups (500 ml/17 fl oz) beef stock and 500 g (1 lb 2 oz) dried pasta elbows after browning the meat and simmer, covered, for 15 minutes.

SERVES 4

Active time
5 minutes

Cooking time
50 minutes

GARLIC CHICKEN DRUMSTICKS

Drumsticks are an affordable family favourite, and they don't need any cutting or trimming at all. In fact, the only thing you're cutting in this recipe is a little garlic. These drumsticks are delicious with steamed rice.

¼ cup (60 ml/2 fl oz) soy sauce
2 tablespoons dark soy sauce
½ cup (175 g/6 oz) honey
¼ cup (60 ml/2 fl oz) apple-cider vinegar
1 kg (2 lb 3 oz) chicken drumsticks
8 garlic cloves, roughly chopped
25 g (1 oz) butter

Heat your oven to 200°C (390°F) fan-forced. Combine the soy sauces, honey and vinegar in a heavy roasting tin big enough to hold the drumsticks, and stir to dissolve the honey. Add the drumsticks and toss to coat in the mixture.

Place the roasting tin into the oven and roast for 45 minutes, turning the drumsticks a few times during cooking. Remove the chicken from the roasting tin and place the tin over medium heat. Add the garlic and butter and cook until the garlic is softened and the sauce has thickened to a glaze.

Spoon the glaze over the chicken, then transfer everything to a serving plate.

Tip

The balance of 'savoury, sweet and sour' is a constant in nearly every cuisine around the world because it tastes great. When trying to cook quickly, simplifying your seasonings to something savoury (soy sauce), sweet (honey) and sour (vinegar) is about as simple as you can get.

SERVES 4

Active time
10 minutes

Cooking time
35 minutes

LAMB KHEEMA

Kheema is a minced (ground) meat curry, which has two benefits for fast cooking: you don't need to cut the meat and it cooks relatively quickly. You can use a food processor or blender to chop the onion, garlic and ginger if you want to speed things along even further.

- 3 tablespoons vegetable oil
- 3 cardamom pods
- 1 cinnamon stick
- 3 cloves
- 1 onion, finely diced
- 4 garlic cloves, roughly chopped
- 2 cm (¾ in) piece fresh ginger, finely chopped
- ¼ cup (60 ml/2 fl oz) tomato passata (puréed tomatoes)
- 1 teaspoon ground turmeric
- 1 teaspoon chilli powder
- salt and black pepper, to season
- 500 g (1 lb 2 oz) minced (ground) lamb
- 1 teaspoon sugar
- 2 tablespoons dried fenugreek leaves (kasuri methi)
- 2 cups (310 g/11 oz) frozen peas
- 15 g (½ oz) butter
- 2 teaspoons garam masala
- 2 tablespoons roughly chopped coriander (cilantro)
- lemon wedges, to serve
- ½ red onion, sliced into rings, to serve
- paratha or rice, to serve
- Indian pickles and chutneys, to serve

Heat a saucepan over medium heat and add the oil, cardamom, cinnamon and cloves. Cook for about 30 seconds until fragrant, then add the onion and fry for a few minutes. Add the garlic and ginger and fry for another few minutes, then add the passata and fry until slightly thickened. Add the turmeric and chilli and mix to combine. Add the lamb and fry for about 5 minutes until browned. Add the sugar and fenugreek and about 1 cup (250 ml/8½ fl oz) water, then cover, reduce the heat to low and simmer for 15 minutes, adding more water if necessary. Add the frozen peas and cook for a further 5 minutes.

Mix through the butter and garam masala, stir through the coriander and squeeze in a couple of wedges of lemon. Serve with onion rings and paratha or rice, and a selection of your favourite Indian pickles and chutneys.

Tip

Like most curries, this dish benefits from being made early to let its flavours develop. You can make it either the day before serving, or make it in the morning and serve it later in the evening.

LESS TIME COOKING

THE 'COOKING' PART OF COOKING – THAT IS TO SAY, THE PART WHERE WE APPLY HEAT TO OUR INGREDIENTS – IS THE PART WE STRESS ABOUT THE MOST. BUT IT'S ALSO THE PART THAT IS THE MOST CONSISTENT WHEN IT COMES TO TIME.

A steak or piece of chicken in a pan in my kitchen will cook in roughly the same amount of time as it will in yours, or your neighbour's, or the pub on the corner's, or in the kitchen of the most expensive restaurant in the world.

Outside of pressure cooking and things like that, reducing your time spent cooking comes down to two main strategies: choose ingredients that cook more quickly, or cut things smaller so that heat can act more quickly on them.

We're mainly talking about meat and seafood here, as nearly all vegetables can be eaten raw (though some legumes require extended cooking). We consider vegetables to be 'done' when we like the texture.

The good news is that most ingredients don't need to be cooked for very long at all, and generally we tend to cook nearly everything for longer than needed. That's a hangover from centuries past, but in a post-nouvelle cuisine (new cooking) world, modern cooking is trending towards shorter cooking times and a fresher, more natural taste in our ingredients.

If you want dishes that don't take too long on the stove, forget braises and ragus. Cuts of meat like beef chuck, lamb shank and chicken drumsticks contain a higher proportion of connective tissue that needs more time on heat for the collagen to be converted to gelatine for a softer texture and richer mouthfeel.

Look instead to cuts like chicken tenderloin or even duck breast, which cook much more quickly, or chicken thighs, which can be sliced thinly without drying out and becoming too tough.

The undisputed champion of quick cooking is seafood. While many meats need to be cooked to internal temperatures of 60–70°C (140–160°F) or even higher, seafood can be considered cooked even in the low 40°Cs (104°Fs).

In this chapter you'll find lots of lightning-fast recipes, using mainly seafood, that spend little more than 10 minutes on the stove.

Choosing dishes like these is very useful if you want to reduce the time you spend in the kitchen. Time at the stove is often the most active, and many of us feel the stress and pressure of cooking most acutely when the heat is on. We peek, stir and adjust constantly to make sure that nothing is burning, and often just to put ourselves at ease.

Dishes that spend just a few minutes on the heat not only reduce the amount of time we spend quite literally over the stove, they also reduce the stress of cooking overall.

96	PRAWN AND LEMON GUAZZETTO
98	QUICK CHICKEN NOODLES
101	SALMON WITH PARSLEY AND DILL SAUCE
103	PAN-ROASTED FLATHEAD WITH PEAS, GREENS AND BACON
104	CRUMBED CHICKEN TENDERS WITH PESTO MAYONNAISE
107	QUICK DUCK À L'ORANGE WITH SARLADAISE POTATOES
109	SPANISH GARLIC PRAWNS
111	STEAMED FLATHEAD WITH SPINACH AND LEMON SAUCE
112	BARBECUED SQUID WITH OREGANO AND PAPRIKA
115	QUICK SRI LANKAN PRAWN CURRY

SERVES 4

Active time
10 minutes

Cooking time
15 minutes

PRAWN AND LEMON GUAZZETTO

Guazzetto is a southern Italian style of cooking that combines olive oil, tomato and wine. Think of it as a light stew. Frying the prawn (shrimp) heads (and then removing them) adds a lot of flavour, but you can skip that part if you don't feel like peeling prawns.

- 600 g whole raw prawns (shrimp), peeled and deveined, heads and shells reserved
- salt and black pepper, to season
- pinch of bicarbonate of soda (baking soda)
- 1 teaspoon fennel seeds
- 4 garlic cloves, bruised
- ½ cup (125 ml/4 fl oz) extra-virgin olive oil
- 1 cup (250 ml/8½ fl oz) white wine
- ½ teaspoon chilli flakes (optional)
- 200 ml (7 fl oz) tomato passata (puréed tomatoes)
- 1 cup (160 g/5½ oz) cherry tomatoes, halved
- 1 small lemon, one half thinly sliced, plus lemon wedges, to serve
- 2 tablespoons finely shredded parsley
- crusty bread, to serve

Butterfly the prawns and season the prawn meat with salt and bicarbonate of soda.

Combine the prawn heads with the fennel seeds, garlic and oil in a large saucepan over medium heat and cook for about 5 minutes until the heads are cooked through and slightly crisp, squeezing the heads to extract as much flavour as possible. Add the wine and bring to a simmer. Remove the prawn heads and discard, then add the chilli, passata and cherry tomatoes.

Add the prawn meat and simmer for about 4 minutes until the prawns are just cooked. Squeeze in the juice of half a lemon, then stir through the sliced lemon and parsley. Transfer to a serving dish, season with black pepper and serve with lemon wedges and crusty bread.

Tip

I've just used the heads as they have the most flavour and are easier to remove from the pan than each individual piece of shell. Don't throw the shells out, though. You can freeze them, make stock or even a delicious prawn oil.

QUICK CHICKEN NOODLES

SERVES 4–6

Active time
10 minutes

Cooking time
10 minutes

This style of fast braising is my preferred way of making noodles. The ingredients are first cooked into a flavourful braise, and then the noodles (that have been microwaved to speed up the process) are added to soak up the sauce as they cook. The simplicity of the process means it's something you'll repeat again and again.

⅓ cup (80 ml/2½ fl oz) vegetable oil

600 g (1 lb 5 oz) boneless chicken thighs, cut into 3 cm (1¼ in) pieces

3 garlic cloves, roughly chopped

1 bunch choy sum, cut into 3 cm (1¼ in) lengths

1 teaspoon chicken stock powder

2 tablespoons oyster sauce

1 tablespoon soy sauce

2 tablespoons dark soy sauce

1 teaspoon sugar

1 kg (2 lb 3 oz) hokkien (egg) noodles

salt and white pepper, to season

6 spring onions (scallions), finely sliced

3 cups (270 g/9½ oz) bean sprouts

chilli sauce, to serve

Heat a Dutch oven over medium heat and add the oil. Add the chicken and fry for about 3 minutes until browned. Add the garlic and fry for about a minute, then add the choy sum and mix well. Add the stock powder, sauces, sugar and 1½ cups (375 ml/12½ fl oz) water. Bring to a simmer. Taste the liquid. It should taste strong and salty (see Tip, below).

While the chicken is simmering, poke a few holes in the pack of noodles and microwave for about 4 minutes. (Check your noodle packet is microwave-safe first.) Massage the bag to break up the noodles, then add to the braising chicken. Toss to coat in the sauce while the noodles absorb the flavour.

Cook for about 3 minutes until the noodles have absorbed all of the liquid. Season with salt and white pepper (if needed). Stir through the spring onion and bean sprouts and serve with chilli sauce.

Tip

The key is making sure the braising liquid is flavourful. It should taste too strong and salty before adding the noodles, so when the unseasoned noodles go in, it all ends up seasoned correctly.

SERVES 4–6

Active time
5 minutes

Cooking time
15 minutes

SALMON WITH PARSLEY AND DILL SAUCE

The nouvelle cuisine movement of the 1960s and 1970s signalled a dramatic change in French cookery, simplifying and lightening dishes, reducing cooking times and making French food healthier in the process. One of the classic dishes of early nouvelle cuisine was salmon with sorrel sauce, created by the legendary Pierre Troisgros. Here I've used parsley and dill in place of sorrel, but the simplicity and elegance of the process remains the same.

30 g (1 oz) butter

1 French shallot, finely minced

½ cup (125 ml/4 fl oz) dry white wine

1 cup (250 ml/8½ fl oz) fish stock or chicken stock

200 ml (7 fl oz) thickened (whipping) cream

salt, to season

¾ cup (25 g/1 oz) roughly chopped flat-leaf (Italian) parsley

¼ cup (15 g/½ oz) roughly chopped dill

2 salmon fillets, about 200 g (7 oz) each, skin removed

lemon wedges, to serve

Heat a frying pan over medium heat, add half the butter and fry the shallot for about 2 minutes until fragrant. Add the wine and bring to a simmer. Simmer until reduced by half. Add the stock and simmer until reduced by half, then add the cream and simmer for 2–3 minutes. Season the sauce well with salt, then stir through the parsley and dill.

While the sauce is simmering, heat a separate frying pan over medium–high heat. Slice the salmon into thin pavé (cobblestones; see Tip, below) around 1–2 cm (½–¾ in) thick by cutting the thin portion of the fillet from the thick portion, and then slicing the thick portion in half horizontally. Season with salt.

Add the remaining butter to the pan and fry the salmon for just a minute on each side until barely cooked and even a little raw in the centre. Place onto a serving plate and pour the sauce over the fillets. Serve with lemon wedges.

Tip

Fish cooks quickly in general, but in this case, we cut the salmon into thin pavé or escalopes that cook even more quickly. Because the fish is so thin, you really don't want to overcook it. Leave it a little raw in the centre as it comes out of the pan and it will cook through as you finish the dish.

PAN-ROASTED FLATHEAD WITH PEAS, GREENS AND BACON

SERVES 4

Active time
10 minutes

Cooking time
15 minutes

A pan-fried piece of fish is one of the simplest and most pleasurable meals that you can have. You don't need to overthink it.

60 g (2 oz) butter

100 g (3½ oz) thick-cut bacon or speck, cut into lardons

2 garlic cloves

1 bunch rainbow chard, cut into 5 cm (2 in) lengths

1 bunch English spinach, cut into 5 cm (2 in) lengths

1 cup (130 g/4½ oz) frozen baby peas

salt and pepper, to season

2 flathead fillets

lemon wedges, to serve

Heat a large frying pan over medium heat and add half the butter. Fry the bacon for about 3 minutes until lightly browned, then add the garlic and fry for a further minute. Add the chard and fry for 2 minutes, then add the spinach and peas and cook for 2–3 minutes until the leafy greens are wilted and the peas are tender. Season well with salt and pepper and transfer to a warm serving plate.

Return the frying pan to medium heat and add a little of the remaining butter. Season the fish well with salt, then fry the fish for about 2 minutes on one side. Flip the fish, add the remaining butter and spoon over the fish for 2–3 minutes as it foams. Remove from the pan and serve with the peas, greens and bacon mixture and a wedge of lemon. Spoon over as much butter from the pan as you feel comfortable with.

Tip

You can of course make this with any other kind of fish fillets you like. Ask your fishmonger for a recommendation if you want to try something new.

SERVES 4

Active time
10 minutes

Cooking time
15 minutes

CRUMBED CHICKEN TENDERS WITH PESTO MAYONNAISE

This recipe uses a clever shortcut, substituting the egg-and-flour process of crumbing with a coating of mayonnaise instead. The mayonnaise does a fantastic job of sticking the breadcrumbs to the chicken, while adding flavour as well.

8 chicken tenderloins

salt and pepper, to season

1 cup (220 g/8 oz) Japanese mayonnaise

1½ cups (90 g/3 oz) panko breadcrumbs

½ cup (125 ml/4 fl oz) vegetable oil, for shallow frying

¼ cup (60 g/2 oz) basil pesto

lemon wedges, to serve

lettuce leaves, to serve

Season the chicken well with salt and pepper. Using about half the mayonnaise, brush it over the chicken, then firmly press the chicken into the breadcrumbs on all sides until well coated.

Heat the oil in a deep frying pan until the temperature reaches 185°C (365°F) and a few crumbs of panko sizzle as soon as they are added to the oil. Add half the chicken and shallow fry for about 2–3 minutes on each side until golden. Remove and drain, then repeat with the remaining chicken.

Mix the remaining mayonnaise with the pesto, and serve with the chicken, lemon wedges, a few leaves of lettuce and a sprinkle of salt.

Tip

When I made this on *The Cook Up*, instead of pesto I made a Yemeni sauce called zhoug by blending together large green chillies, red bird's eye chillies, fresh coriander (cilantro) and parsley, garlic and ground cumin and coriander with plenty of olive oil.

QUICK DUCK À L'ORANGE WITH SARLADAISE POTATOES

SERVES 4

Active time
10 minutes

Cooking time
20 minutes

Resting time
5–10 minutes

Duck à l'orange might not seem like the kind of thing you'd choose to make for a quick dinner, but trust me. Duck breasts themselves are very easy to cook, and in the process, you render duck fat that can be used for some quick potatoes. This dish is about smart process, and when the process is smart you can achieve a lot more in the kitchen than you might have thought possible.

2 duck breasts
salt, to season
6 thyme sprigs

SARLADAISE POTATOES

400 g (14 oz) washed potatoes, cut into 1 cm (½ in) slices
4 garlic cloves, thinly sliced
salt, to season
2 tablespoons finely chopped parsley

ORANGE SAUCE

¼ cup (55 g/2 oz) sugar
2 tablespoons sherry vinegar
juice and julienned zest of 1 orange
1 cup (250 ml/8½ fl oz) chicken stock
1 teaspoon powdered gelatine
25 g (1 oz) cold butter, cut into cubes
1 small orange, extra, segmented

Season the duck breasts well with salt and place, skin-side down, in a cold, dry frying pan. Place a cooking weight on top. Add the thyme. Place the pan over low–medium heat and cook for 15 minutes until the fat is rendered and the duck is cooked to medium-rare. Remove the duck and set aside in a warm place to rest for 5–10 minutes.

To make the sarladaise potatoes, add the potatoes to the rendered fat in the pan and fry for about 3 minutes until lightly golden. Add the garlic and continue to fry for another minute or two until the potatoes are deeply golden. Add 2 tablespoons water and season well with salt. Cover and cook the potatoes for about 5 minutes until they are tender and the water has evaporated. Season with salt again and stir through the parsley.

To make the orange sauce, heat the sugar and 1 tablespoon water in a frying pan until it starts to caramelise to a light golden brown. Add the vinegar and orange juice and mix well. Add the stock, gelatine and zest and simmer for 5–10 minutes until reduced to the consistency of maple syrup. Whisk in the butter, then taste and season. Stir through the orange segments.

Slice the duck and serve with the sauce and the potatoes.

Tip

Powdered gelatine is a great addition to sauces. Commercial stocks often have much of the gelatine removed so that they don't solidify in the fridge, but gelatine is important for mouthfeel, so adding a spoon to your sauce will give it a better texture.

SERVES 4–6

Active time
5 minutes

Cooking time
10 minutes

SPANISH GARLIC PRAWNS
Gambas al ajillo

It's always amazing to me how a dish that is so simple can taste so good. It's a Spanish classic for a reason. Just don't overcook the prawns (shrimp). Please.

- 750 g whole raw prawns (shrimp), peeled and deveined with tails on and shells reserved
- ¾ cup (180 ml/6 fl oz) extra-virgin olive oil
- salt, to season
- ¼ teaspoon bicarbonate of soda (baking soda)
- 6 garlic cloves, sliced
- 2 dried red chillies
- 2 teaspoons dry sherry or brandy
- 1 tablespoon finely shredded parsley
- crusty baguette, to serve

Combine the prawn shells with the oil in a large saucepan over medium heat and cook for about 5 minutes until the shells are cooked through and slightly crisp, squeezing the heads to extract as much flavour as possible. Pour the oil through a strainer into a clean saucepan.

While the shells are cooking, butterfly the prawns and season the prawn meat with salt and bicarbonate of soda. Set aside for 10 minutes.

Heat the pan with the prawn oil over medium heat. Add the garlic and fry for about 4 minutes until very lightly browned. Add the chillies and prawns and fry for about 4 minutes until the prawns are just barely cooked. Add the sherry and toss through the parsley. Transfer to a serving dish and serve with crusty bread.

Tip

Bicarbonate of soda added to a marinade increases the pH, which reduces the amount of protein bonding. For prawns, this helps to keep them crisp and tender, and gives you more of a safety net in cooking to avoid the rubbery texture of overcooked prawns.

SERVES 4

Active time
10 minutes

Cooking time
30 minutes

STEAMED FLATHEAD WITH SPINACH AND LEMON SAUCE

Steaming is one of the gentlest ways to cook fish. If you have a steam oven, it's also one of the easiest. If you don't, this can easily be made in a bamboo steamer over a pot of simmering water.

4 potatoes, peeled

2 flathead fillets

salt, to season

SPINACH AND LEMON SAUCE

150 g (5½ oz) butter, cubed and chilled

½ small onion, finely diced

2 garlic cloves, roughly chopped

½ cup (125 ml/4 fl oz) white wine

2 teaspoons fish sauce

120 g (4½ oz) baby spinach

1 cup (60 g/2 oz) loosely packed parsley

½ cup (125 ml/4 fl oz) seafood or chicken stock

juice of ½ lemon, plus lemon wedges to serve

salt and pepper, to season

Steam the potatoes for 20 minutes until very tender using your preferred method of steaming. Remove, quarter and set aside. Add the flathead to the steamer and steam for 6 minutes. Remove and season with salt.

To make the sauce, place one-quarter of the butter in a small saucepan over medium heat and add the onion and garlic. Cook for 3–4 minutes until fragrant, then add the wine and bring to a simmer. Simmer until the wine is reduced by half, then add the fish sauce, spinach and parsley and cook until wilted. Add the stock and bring to a simmer. Simmer for 1 minute, then transfer to a high-speed blender, add the lemon juice and purée until smooth. Add the remaining butter, a few cubes at a time, to produce a smooth sauce. Season well with salt and pepper.

Place the flathead on a serving plate and pour over the sauce. Serve with the potatoes and lemon wedges, and season with salt and pepper.

Tip

If your sauce doesn't look thick enough, you can thicken it with a little cornflour (cornstarch) and cold water.

BARBECUED SQUID WITH OREGANO AND PAPRIKA

SERVES 4

Active time
10 minutes

Cooking time
10 minutes

Simplicity is the key to this dish. Simple seasonings you probably have in your pantry right now combined with a very simple cooking process make for a very simple dinner. Good olive oil is a must.

2 medium potatoes, peeled and cut into 1 cm (½ in) slices

1 large plate-sized squid, cleaned (see Tip, below) but whole (or 2–3 small squid)

salt and black pepper, to season

1 teaspoon Greek oregano

1 teaspoon smoked paprika

2 tablespoons very good quality extra-virgin olive oil, plus extra to serve

lemon wedges, to serve

Place the potatoes in a covered microwave-safe dish and add 1 tablespoon water. Microwave for 5 minutes and check for doneness. They should be very tender. If not, microwave for additional 1–2 minute intervals until cooked to your liking.

Cut thick slits into the top of the squid tube (the side furthest from the fins). Scatter with salt and pepper, and a little of the oregano and paprika, and drizzle with oil. Set aside while you heat your barbecue or chargrill pan over high heat.

Grill the squid with the slits facing up and a cooking weight placed on top, or pressing with the back of a spatula, for 2–3 minutes. Hold the joints of the wings and body against the grill for a few seconds on each side. Flip and grill the top side until cooked through.

Transfer the squid and potatoes to a serving plate and drizzle with extra olive oil, more salt and pepper, oregano and paprika. Squeeze over a little lemon juice and serve with wedges of lemon.

Tip

To clean the squid, remove the head and tentacles, cut off the eyes and remove the beak. Remove everything from the cavity, including the cartilage, and rinse well. Peel the skin off by hand and rub the suckers to remove the cartilage from within the suckers. Or just get your fishmonger to do all that.

SERVES 4

Active time
5 minutes

Cooking time
15 minutes

QUICK SRI LANKAN PRAWN CURRY

We often think of curries as dishes that stew for a long time, but the southern parts of the Indian subcontinent produce delicious seafood dishes that cook very quickly by comparison. The first step is to get the sauce or gravy right, then the seafood is added to cook in the last few minutes.

- 2 tablespoons vegetable oil
- ½ teaspoon yellow mustard seeds
- ½ teaspoon fennel seeds
- 2 cardamom pods
- 5 cloves
- 10 cm (4 in) pandan leaf (about ½ a leaf; optional)
- 10 curry leaves
- 2 onions, peeled and sliced
- 2 garlic cloves, roughly chopped
- 2 cm (¾ in) ginger, peeled and julienned
- 1 large green chilli, sliced
- 1 teaspoon ground turmeric
- 2 teaspoons ground coriander
- 1 teaspoon garam masala
- ½ teaspoon ground cumin
- ¼ teaspoon ground black pepper
- 1 teaspoon salt
- ½ teaspoon sugar
- 200 ml (7 fl oz) coconut cream
- 600 g (1 lb 5 oz) raw prawns (shrimp), peeled and deveined with tails on
- juice of 1 lemon
- steamed rice, to serve

Heat a large saucepan over medium heat and add the oil. Add the mustard and fennel seeds and the cardamom and cloves. Cook for about 30 seconds until the seeds crackle, then snip in the pandan leaf in 2 cm (¾ in) lengths, if using, and add the curry leaves, onion, garlic, ginger and chilli. Fry for about 3 minutes until softened and fragrant, then add the turmeric, coriander, garam masala, cumin, pepper, salt and sugar, and stir well.

Add 1 cup (250 ml/8½ fl oz) water and the coconut cream, then stir and bring to a simmer. Cook for 5 minutes, then stir through the prawns and cook for a further 3 minutes. Stir through the lemon juice and serve with rice.

Tip

The final addition of lemon juice adds a lovely freshness to the dish. You could also use lime juice or a dash of vinegar.

LESS TIME WASHING

THE ENDURING APPEAL OF ONE-POT DISHES IS EASY TO UNDERSTAND. THE POT IS LIKE A MAGICIAN'S HAT: YOU THROW IN A BUNCH OF INGREDIENTS, WAVE YOUR WAND, AND DINNER APPEARS IN A PUFF OF SMOKE. BEST OF ALL, THE ONLY THING LEFT TO DO IS WASH A SINGLE POT.

Washing up is the part of cooking that gets little love in popular culture. It's never written into recipes, it doesn't feature in cooking shows, and most chefs never talk about it (because most chefs aren't the ones who actually end up doing it!).

When we were first creating *The Cook Up*, I did suggest that the end sequence of each episode should be a single, long shot of the dishes being done. Apparently nobody but me thought that would make good television.

Even if the arrangement in your household is that common bargain where the person who cooks doesn't have to wash up, reducing the amount of dishes that need to be washed is always going to be welcome.

My grandmother was the best cook I've ever known and one of the things I remember most vividly from her cooking is that at every stage the kitchen was completely clean. There was never a sink overflowing with dishes or a kitchen looking like a bomb site. Her kitchen always looked like what it was – the well-ordered space of someone who really knew what she was doing.

I consider a clean kitchen to be the mark of good cooking, and when I'm cooking well my kitchen is ordered and organised. I don't always get it right, and sometimes it devolves to a more chaotic state.

It might not be immediately apparent, but there is a pretty reliable connection between a clean kitchen and good food. If your kitchen is clean, you're in control, and if you're in control you have the time to get your cooking right.

The recipes in this chapter are ones that help you stay in control of your cooking by reducing the amount of washing you need to do. Traybakes, one-pot wonders and all-in roasts are excellent for keeping your head in the kitchen. They might not cook quickly, but once the lid is on the pot or the oven door is closed, there's little more for you to do than tidy up and wait.

120	**MANGALOREAN PORK MASALA**
122	**ORANGE AND FENNEL CHICKEN TRAYBAKE**
125	**COLCANNON RISOTTO**
127	**BAKED TUSCAN CHICKEN**
129	**TURKISH ROAST LAMB SHOULDER**
130	**CREAMY CHICKEN, LEEK AND MUSHROOM STEW**
133	**MUSHROOM CACCIATORE**
134	**HONEY MUSTARD CHICKEN CUTLETS**
137	**WHOLE BAKED FISH WITH VADOUVAN BUTTER**
138	**SOY SAUCE CHICKEN WITH SPRING ONION OIL**
141	**HAWAIIAN SHOYU CHICKEN**

SERVES 4

Active time
10 minutes

Cooking time
1 hour 30 minutes

Resting time
1 hour

MANGALOREAN PORK MASALA
Dukra maas

This curry from the west coast of India couldn't be easier – just throw everything into a single pot to marinate and cook it together. Make sure to use a non-reactive pot, as the acidic vinegar used to marinate may react with some materials.

- 2 kg (4 lb 6 oz) pork belly, cut into 2 cm (¾ in) cubes
- 2 green chillies, halved
- 10 garlic cloves, bruised
- 5 cm (2 in) piece fresh ginger, finely minced
- 1 cassia or cinnamon stick
- 6 cloves
- 3 bay leaves
- 1 tablespoon ground cumin
- 1 tablespoon ground coriander
- 1 tablespoon ground turmeric
- 1 teaspoon Kashmiri or Korean chilli powder (or to taste)
- 1 teaspoon ground black pepper
- 2 tablespoons tamarind paste
- 2 tablespoons white vinegar
- 1 tablespoon sugar
- 1 teaspoon salt (or to taste)
- 4 onions, diced

Combine all the ingredients except the onion in a large pot and mix to combine. Set aside for 1 hour.

Place the pot over medium–high heat, add 1 cup (250 ml/8½ fl oz) water and bring to a simmer. Reduce the heat to low, cover and cook for 1 hour. Add the onion, stir and cook for another 30 minutes until the onions have softened and the pork is very tender. Serve.

Tip

This version uses individual spices but it's traditionally made with 'bafat powder', a kind of masala spice mix with Portuguese influences found in Goan and Mangalorean cuisines. If you can find it at your local Indian grocer feel free to use that instead.

SERVES 6

Active time
5 minutes

Cooking time
45 minutes

Resting time
5 minutes

ORANGE AND FENNEL CHICKEN TRAYBAKE

Orange and fennel are a match made in heaven. Here we're using fennel bulb and seeds, for two different expressions of its slightly aniseed taste. Both are from the same plant – *Foeniculum vulgare* – but the vegetable is a cultivar of the original plant selected for a larger, more tender base of the leaves forming the bulb.

6 chicken thigh cutlets (bone-in, skin on)

½ cup (125 ml/4 fl oz) soy sauce

½ cup (175 g/6 oz) honey

juice and grated zest of 1 orange

1 teaspoon grated ginger

1 teaspoon fennel seeds

2 onions, cut into thick wedges

1 fennel bulb, cut into thick wedges

¼ cup (60 ml/2 fl oz) olive oil

salt and black pepper, to season

Combine the chicken, soy sauce, honey, orange juice and zest, ginger and fennel seeds in a bowl and mix to combine.

Heat your oven to 200°C (390°F) fan-forced and line a roasting tin with baking paper. Combine the onion, fresh fennel and oil in a large bowl and toss to combine, then arrange in the prepared tin. Place the chicken in the same roasting tin, pour over any extra marinade in the bowl and season with salt and black pepper. Roast in the oven for 45 minutes. Allow to stand for 5 minutes, then serve.

Tip

Grating zest is easy. Use a microplane grater and work your way methodically around the orange (or lemon or lime). Do this before cutting it and juicing will be much easier. If you don't have a microplane or zester, just leave the zest out.

COLCANNON RISOTTO

SERVES 4–6

Active time
10 minutes

Cooking time
20 minutes

Risotto is a dish that has changed a lot in Australia. In the 1990s, when it started to become popular, most Aussie risottos were chunky and solid, with grains mashed together from constant stirring. These days I prefer risotto to have separate grains and to spread more easily on the plate.

6 cups (1.5 litres/51 fl oz) vegetable stock

¼ cup (60 ml/2 fl oz) olive oil

1 small onion, finely diced

3 garlic cloves, sliced

2 cups (370 g/13 oz) arborio or other risotto rice

½ cup (125 ml/4 fl oz) white wine

25 g (1 oz) butter, plus extra to serve

½ cup (50 g/1¾ oz) grated pecorino or parmesan, plus extra to serve

salt and pepper, to season

GREENS

25 g (1 oz) butter

1 tablespoon olive oil

1 cup (75 g/2¾ oz) thinly sliced brussels sprouts

2 cups (150 g/5½ oz) roughly chopped kale

½ cup (30 g/1 oz) finely sliced spring onions (scallions)

1 tablespoon finely shredded parsley, plus extra to serve

Place the stock in a small saucepan and bring to a simmer. Heat a large casserole dish over medium heat and add the oil and onion. Fry the onion for about 3 minutes until translucent, then add the garlic and fry for a further minute. Add the rice and toast in the oil for about a minute, then add the wine and stir until absorbed. Add the stock and simmer for about 12 minutes until the rice is al dente.

While the rice is cooking, make the greens. Heat a large frying pan over medium heat and add the butter, oil and brussels sprouts. Cook for about a minute or two until starting to colour, then add the kale, spring onion and parsley and fry until the kale is wilted.

When the rice is ready, vigorously stir through the butter and pecorino to create a creamy risotto. Taste and adjust the seasoning. The texture of the risotto should be quite soft so that it spreads easily on a plate if you tap the bottom of the plate. Use some extra stock or water to thin the risotto if the texture looks too firm. Stir the greens through the risotto. Scatter with more pecorino, pepper and parsley, and serve with a bit more melted butter poured on top.

Tip

You don't need to stir risotto constantly. You just don't. The creaminess of risotto comes from the mantecatura, which simply means to stir at the end, emulsifying the oil from the butter and cheese into the starch from the rice.

SERVES 6

Active time
5 minutes

Cooking time
40 minutes

BAKED TUSCAN CHICKEN

If you want an endorsement for this dish, here's one from my seven-year-old daughter, Anna, who tried it for the first time tonight (as I sit here editing the recipe). Her review: 'Wow, Dad! That's actually pretty great!'

6 chicken thigh cutlets (bone-in, skin on)

salt and black pepper, to season

2 tablespoons olive oil

2 onions, sliced

4 garlic cloves, sliced

200 g (7 oz) sun-dried tomatoes, sliced

60 g (2 oz) baby spinach leaves

300 ml (10 fl oz) thickened (whipping) cream

½ cup (50 g/1¾ oz) grated parmesan cheese

2 teaspoons dried Italian seasoning, or 1 teaspoon each dried oregano and thyme

Heat your oven to 180°C (360°F) fan-forced. Season the chicken well with salt and pepper. Heat a heavy ovenproof pan over medium heat. Add the oil and fry the chicken, skin-side down first, until nicely browned on both sides. Remove from the pan. Add the onion and garlic and fry for 3 minutes until lightly browned.

Add the tomato, spinach, cream, parmesan and Italian seasoning and place the chicken on top, skin up. Transfer to the oven and bake for 25 minutes, uncovered, until the chicken is cooked through and the sauce is thickened and reduced.

Tip

A good rule of thumb is that if a dish has the name of a place in the title, it's not from that place. This is no exception. It's an American dish, and it's named 'Tuscan chicken' presumably because of the Italian-ish ingredients and the fact that Tuscany has kind of a nice vibe.

SERVES 6–8

Active time
15 minutes

Cooking time
4 hours

Resting time
15 minutes

TURKISH ROAST LAMB SHOULDER

This vaguely Turkish-inspired lamb shoulder takes some cues from kuzu tandir, a Turkish lamb dish notable for its tender, fall-apart texture. Make this on a Saturday or Sunday, when you can get the lamb in the oven after lunch and forget about it until dinner.

3 tablespoons olive oil

juice of ½ lemon

2 tablespoons Turkish red pepper paste (biber salçasi), or tomato paste (concentrated purée)

1 teaspoon dried oregano

1 tablespoon ground cumin

1 tablespoon smoked paprika

salt and black pepper, to season

1.5 kg (3 lb 5 oz) lamb shoulder, bone-in

1 garlic bulb, halved horizontally

sliced tomato, to serve

butter lettuce leaves, to serve

Turkish-style pickled chillies, to serve

pita or flour tortillas, to serve

SUMAC ONIONS

2 red onions, thinly sliced into rounds

1 teaspoon sumac

salt, to season

2 tablespoons roughly chopped parsley

MINT YOGHURT

1 cup (20 g/¾ oz) loosely packed mint, shredded

2 cups (500 g/1 lb 2 oz) thick Greek-style yoghurt

olive oil, for drizzling

Combine the oil, lemon juice, red pepper paste and dried herbs and spices, season very well with salt and pepper and rub all over the lamb shoulder.

Heat your oven to 180°C (360°F) conventional. Place the garlic in the base of a large casserole dish and add 1 cup (250 ml/8½ fl oz) water. Place the lamb on top, cover with a lid and roast in the oven for 3 hours. Remove the lid and cook for a further hour until the lamb is very tender. Set aside to rest for at least 15 minutes.

To make the sumac onions, toss the onion in the sumac and season with salt. Scatter with chopped parsley.

To make the mint yoghurt, stir the mint into the yoghurt and drizzle with olive oil.

Serve the lamb with a platter of sliced tomato, lettuce leaves, pickled chillies and the sumac onions, with the pita and mint yoghurt on the side.

Tip

Lamb shoulder is a very forgiving cut. It has surpassed leg as Australia's favourite kind of roast lamb, likely because it can be thrown in the oven and left alone to do its thing. It doesn't need to be cooked for a long time, though. If you prefer it medium-rare, cook it at the same temperature, uncovered, for about an hour.

CREAMY CHICKEN, LEEK AND MUSHROOM STEW

SERVES 4

Active time
10 minutes

Cooking time
25 minutes

This simple white chicken stew can be varied in lots of different ways. Switch the leeks out for onions if leeks are too expensive. Exchange the mushrooms for a few handfuls of baby spinach, or some diced pumpkin (squash), or just leave them out entirely.

- ¼ cup (35 g/1¼ oz) plain (all-purpose) flour
- salt and pepper, to season
- 1.5 kg (3 lb 5 oz) boneless chicken thighs (around 6)
- 2 tablespoons olive oil
- 20 g (¾ oz) butter
- 300 g (10½ oz) button mushrooms, sliced
- 2–3 leeks, cut into 1 cm (½ in) rounds
- 2 garlic cloves, roughly chopped
- 3 rosemary sprigs
- 1 fresh bay leaf, or 2 dried
- ½ cup (125 ml/4 fl oz) white wine
- 1 cup (250 ml/8½ fl oz) chicken stock
- 200 ml (7 fl oz) thickened (whipping) cream
- chopped parsley, to serve

Season the flour very well with salt and pepper, then dust the chicken with the flour. Heat a shallow casserole dish over medium heat and add the oil and butter. Brown the chicken thighs in batches for a few minutes each side, then remove from the pan. They don't have to be cooked through. While the chicken is cooking, microwave the mushrooms for 5 minutes.

Add the mushroom to the casserole dish and fry until lightly browned. Add the leek, garlic, rosemary, bay leaf and any remaining flour from the dusting and fry for a few minutes. Add the wine and scrape any brown bits from the base of the casserole dish, simmering until the wine stops smelling alcoholic.

Return the chicken to the pot and add the stock and cream. Bring to a simmer, cover and reduce the heat to low and cook the chicken for 10 minutes. Season well with salt and pepper. Scatter with parsley to serve.

Tip

I've suggested 1 cup (250 ml/8½ fl oz) chicken stock here because chicken can often release quite a lot of liquid (its own 'stock') through the cooking process. Adjust the quantities of liquid up or down depending on how thick or thin you want the stew to be.

MUSHROOM CACCIATORE

SERVES 4

Active time
10 minutes

Cooking time
1 hour 5 minutes

Resting time
10 minutes

Cacciatore is a 'hunter'-style braise popularly made with chicken or rabbit, but there's not a lot of hunting that goes into this mushroom version.

1 kg (2 lb 3 oz) button mushrooms

½ cup (125 ml/4 fl oz) olive oil

2 onions, thickly sliced

3 garlic cloves, roughly chopped

1 red capsicum (bell pepper), sliced

½ cup (75 g/2¾ oz) sun-dried tomatoes, finely chopped

400 g (14 oz) tinned whole cherry tomatoes

125 ml (4 fl oz) red wine

1 teaspoon vegetable stock

2 tablespoons tomato sauce (ketchup)

3 bay leaves

3 thyme sprigs

salt and black pepper, to season

½ cup (80 g/2¾ oz) pitted kalamata olives

¼ cup (15 g/½ oz) finely shredded parsley, to serve

POLENTA

1 cup (150 g/5½ oz) fine polenta

75 g (2¾ oz) butter

½ cup (50 g/1¾ oz) finely grated parmesan cheese

Heat your oven to 200°C (390°F) fan-forced. Microwave the mushrooms for 5 minutes. Heat a wide casserole dish over medium heat and add the oil. Fry the mushrooms for about 5 minutes until lightly browned, then remove from the pan, reserving any liquid.

Add the onion and stir for a few minutes until lightly browned, then add the garlic, capsicum, sun-dried tomatoes, cherry tomatoes, wine, stock, tomato sauce, bay leaves, thyme and season well with salt and pepper. Return the mushrooms to the pot and add the olives. Place in the oven uncovered for 30 minutes, then rest for 10 minutes.

To make the polenta, bring 5 cups (1.25 litres/42 fl oz) water to the boil in a large saucepan and whisk in the polenta. Whisk for a couple more minutes then reduce the heat to very low and simmer, partially covered, for 30 minutes. Whisk in the butter and parmesan. Thin with a little water if too thick.

Spoon the polenta on to plates and top with the cacciatore. Sprinkle with parsley to serve.

Tip

You've probably seen a few recipes in this book where I ask you to microwave your mushrooms and perhaps you've wondered why. It's a great time saver, because microwaving collapses the air spaces in the mushrooms so they don't absorb too much oil and can fry much more quickly.

SERVES 6

Active time
5 minutes

Cooking time
45 minutes

Resting time
5 minutes

HONEY MUSTARD CHICKEN CUTLETS

Honey and mustard are a great combination because the sweetness of honey helps to balance the sourness and slight bitterness of the mustard.

3 red onions, cut into wedges

¼ cup (60 ml/2 fl oz) olive oil

¼ cup (90 g/3 oz) honey

¼ cup (60 g/2 oz) dijon mustard

1 tablespoon white-wine vinegar

½ teaspoon salt

10 thyme sprigs, leaves stripped

6 chicken thigh cutlets (bone-in, skin on)

black pepper, to season

Heat your oven to 200°C (390°F) fan-forced and line a roasting tin with baking paper.

Toss the onion in the oil in a large bowl and arrange in the prepared tin, leaving any remaining oil in the bowl. Add the honey, mustard, vinegar, salt and thyme to the bowl and mix to combine. Roll the chicken thighs through the mixture and place in the roasting tin with the onions.

Pour in any remaining mixture, season with black pepper and roast in the oven for 45 minutes. Allow to stand for 5 minutes, then serve.

Tip

One really great thing about traybakes is that they are easily scalable both up and down, and you don't have to change the cooking time. If you've got more people, just use more chicken and onions and put them in a bigger roasting tin.

WHOLE BAKED FISH WITH VADOUVAN BUTTER

SERVES 4

Active time
10 minutes

Cooking time
20 minutes

People are terrified of whole fish because they think there'll be a lot of scaling, cleaning and filleting needed to make it happen. Not at all. Ask your fishmonger to scale and clean your fish (they probably have already). Fish comes off the bone much more easily after being cooked so no filleting required. All you have to do is put it on a tray and pop it in the oven.

1 plate-sized Murray cod or snapper (about 800 g/1 lb 12 oz), cleaned

2 tablespoons vegetable oil

100 g (3½ oz) unsalted butter

3 French shallots, sliced

2 cm (¾ in) fresh ginger, peeled and finely sliced

3 garlic cloves, sliced

1 sprig curry leaves

lime wedges, to serve (optional)

 VADOUVAN CURRY POWDER (MAKES EXTRA)

15 curry leaves

1 teaspoon fenugreek seeds

1 tablespoon cumin seeds

2 tablespoons coriander seeds

3 green cardamom pods

1 teaspoon black peppercorns

1 teaspoon brown mustard seeds

1½ teaspoons ground turmeric

2 dried red chillies

6 cloves

Heat your oven to 180°C (360°F) fan-forced and line a baking tray with baking paper. Place the fish on the prepared tray, drizzle with the oil and bake for 15 minutes.

To make the curry powder, combine all the ingredients in a small saucepan over medium heat and cook, swirling, for about 2 minutes until fragrant. Grind to a fine powder in a spice grinder or small food processor.

Return the saucepan to the heat and add the butter. Fry the shallot, ginger and garlic until the mixture is fragrant and the butter is starting to brown, then add the curry leaves and 2 teaspoons of the curry powder. Cook for a further minute, then remove from the heat. Transfer the fish to a serving plate and pour over the vadouvan butter. Serve with lime wedges.

Tip

Vadouvan is a French curry powder, and if you make your own for this recipe it will keep in an airtight container for about a month before it loses a lot of its aroma. If you don't want to go to the effort of making your own curry powder, just use your favourite blend.

SOY SAUCE CHICKEN WITH SPRING ONION OIL

SERVES 6

Active time
10 minutes

Cooking time
55 minutes

Resting time
15 minutes

This is a classic Cantonese-style 'lo sui' dish that is frankly so incredibly easy it feels like cheating. This braising liquid is sometimes called 'master stock' in English, but I've never called it that (or heard any other Chinese person call it that either). The chicken is simmered at very low heat so that it is gently cooked and impossibly tender.

6 chicken leg quarters

 SOY SAUCE BRAISE (LO SUI)

2 cups (500 ml/17 fl oz) soy sauce

1 cup (250 ml/8½ fl oz) dark soy sauce

1 onion, halved and with the skin on

1 thumb-sized knob of fresh ginger, thickly sliced

2 star anise

2 cinnamon sticks

1 piece dried tangerine peel

1½ cups (345 g/2 oz) caster (superfine) sugar

 SPRING ONION OIL (MAKES EXTRA)

2 tablespoons grated ginger

5 spring onions (scallions), white and light green parts, thinly sliced

½ teaspoon salt flakes

½ cup (125 ml/4 fl oz) vegetable oil

Combine all the ingredients for the soy sauce braise in a very large pot and pour in 4 cups (1 litre/34 fl oz) water. Bring to the boil, stirring to dissolve the sugar. Add the chicken and reduce the heat to very low. Cover and simmer for 45 minutes. Turn off the heat and allow the chicken to cool in the liquid for a further 15 minutes.

Transfer 2 cups (500 ml/17 fl oz) of the poaching liquid to a small frying pan and bring to the boil. Cook for about 5 minutes or until reduced by about half.

To make the spring onion oil, pound the ginger, spring onion and salt to a coarse paste in a heatproof mortar. Heat the oil in a small saucepan over high heat until smoking and pour over the mixture.

If you can, remove the chicken from the bone and cut into slices. Serve with the reduced poaching liquid and spring onion oil.

Tip

If there's one thing you take from this book, it should be this braising liquid. After the chicken has been removed, you can bring the braising liquid to the boil, allow it to cool, and freeze it for poaching again another time – chicken, pork, beef or any other meat or seafood. Every few times you use it, just add a little extra soy sauce, salt and/or sugar to maintain the seasoning, but you can just eyeball that.

SERVES 4

Active time
5 minutes

Cooking time
25 minutes

HAWAIIAN SHOYU CHICKEN

This Hawaiian dish is a blend of Japanese-style teriyaki and Filipino-style adobo. It's one of the most popular recipes we've ever had on *The Cook Up*.

1 tablespoon vegetable oil

6 chicken thigh cutlets (bone-in, skin on)

½ cup (125 ml/4 fl oz) soy sauce

½ cup (115 g/4 oz) sugar

¼ cup (60 ml/2 fl oz) rice vinegar

3 garlic cloves, smashed

2 cm (¾ in) piece fresh ginger, sliced

3 spring onions (scallions), finely sliced

1 tablespoon toasted sesame seeds

Heat a large, lidded frying pan over medium heat. Fry the chicken, skin-side down, for about 6 minutes until well browned, then turn skin-side up and add the soy sauce, sugar, vinegar, garlic and ginger and about ½ cup (125 ml/4 fl oz) water.

Bring to a simmer, stirring to dissolve the sugar. Spoon the sauce over the top of the chicken, cover and simmer for 10 minutes until the chicken is cooked. Remove the chicken from the pan and boil the sauce until thick enough to coat a spoon. Spoon the sauce over the chicken and scatter generously with the spring onions and sesame seeds to serve.

Tip

When you're frying chicken with the skin on, it can spit a little. Use a splatter guard, or just place a paper towel directly on top of the chicken as it browns to stop the spitting oil. After you've turned the chicken and added the sauces it will stop spitting, and you can remove the paper towel.

1

WHILE THE PASTA COOKS

PASTA IS A LIFESAVER FOR SPEEDY COOKING. IT SITS IN YOUR PANTRY, READY TO BE TURNED INTO A DELICIOUS MEAL AT A MOMENT'S NOTICE. WHOEVER INVENTED DRIED PASTA ALL THOSE YEARS AGO DID US A GREAT SERVICE.

I love a spaghetti bolognese (who doesn't?), but if the only pastas in your repertoire are slow-cooked ragus and braises then you're going to struggle when you've got to get dinner on the table in a hurry.

Thankfully, there are many pasta dishes that don't require hours of cooking. In this chapter I've collected some great recipes that will all cook in the time it takes to boil the pasta.

The first thing you need to get your thinking around is that most pasta dishes are not about boiling some pasta and plonking a few spoonfuls of sauce on top. In fact, they're not really about sauce at all. The key to a great pasta is combining the ingredients with the pasta as a single dish.

This might sound strange, but I often think of making pasta as a bit like stir-frying. Stir-frying is mostly about seasoning the natural flavours of the ingredients, and then adjusting the consistency at the end by tossing the wok and using a starch slurry to emulsify the oils from cooking with the natural juices of the ingredients.

That same process of emulsification is the key to great pasta. It's known in Italian as mantecatura – the process of finishing a risotto with cheese or butter, or mixing pasta with some of the starchy pasta water to emulsify the oil used in cooking – and it produces a luxurious risotto or a saucy consistency to coat the pasta.

You'll find different oils are used in these pastas. Olive oil is the main one, but there is also butter, the oils contained in cheeses, and the oil that renders from frying bacon or pancetta. All of them emulsify with the pasta and the starchy pasta water at the end of the cooking process to create your 'sauce'.

The recipes in this chapter use a 500 g (1 lb 2 oz) packet of dried pasta. I know that's more than some of you will need, but I consider it a standard measurement as that's the most common weight of a packet of dried pasta in Australia. Just cook it all. This stops you having half a packet left over in the pantry for weeks or months on end, and when it comes to efficiency in cooking, it's much better to have leftovers than to have to cook again.

To cook 500 g (1 lb 2 oz) pasta, you need a large pan that can combine all the pasta and ingredients, with enough room to move it about a bit. I have a large 33 cm (13 in) diameter 'chef pan' that I use for all my pasta dishes. It's a double-handled pan a little deeper than a standard frying pan that I use for cooking the ingredients while the pasta boils in a large saucepan. Then I transfer the pasta to the pan with tongs (for long pasta) or a mesh scoop (for short pasta) and add ladles of the pasta water as needed.

I also cook dried pasta for 2 minutes less than it says on the packet. This allows me to finish cooking the pasta to al dente with the other ingredients, so that it absorbs their flavour and gets coated by the 'sauce' in the process of mantecatura.

146	TOMATO AND CAPSICUM PENNE
149	PACCHERI WITH PANCETTA AND PISTACHIO
151	SPAGHETTI VONGOLE ROSSO
152	CHICKEN AND CREAM CHEESE PENNE
155	TINNED FISH WITH CAPERS AND TOMATO SPAGHETTI
157	LINGUINE WITH MUSSELS AND PANCETTA
158	PASTA ALLA CARLOFORTINA
161	'ANTIPASTA'
162	PANTRY PASTA
165	CREAMY LEMON PASTA

TOMATO AND CAPSICUM PENNE

SERVES 4–6

Active time
10 minutes

Cooking time
35 minutes

A simple tomato pasta is fantastic as it is – simply cooked tomato passata (puréed tomatoes) tossed with pasta and olive oil and finished with parmesan and perhaps a bit of basil. But if you want to level that up a little, this blended sauce of capsicum (bell pepper) and tomato is a great choice.

500 g (1 lb 2 oz) penne

½ cup (125 ml/4 fl oz) olive oil

1 onion, roughly chopped

1 red capsicum (bell pepper), roughly chopped

6 garlic cloves, roughly chopped

1 bird's eye chilli

700 ml (23½ fl oz) tomato passata (puréed tomatoes)

½ cup (50 g/1¾ oz) freshly grated parmesan cheese

75 g (2¾ oz) butter, cold and cubed

SMOKED PAPRIKA OIL (MAKES EXTRA)

1 cup (250 ml/8½ fl oz) olive oil

2 tablespoons smoked paprika

2 teaspoons gochugaru (Korean chilli powder)

To make the smoked paprika oil, heat the oil in a small saucepan over low heat until warm and add the paprika and chilli. Cook for about 10 minutes, taking care not to burn the spices. Strain through a fine sieve and discard the solids. Set aside.

Bring a large saucepan of salted water to the boil. Add the pasta and cook according to the packet directions, checking about 2 minutes before the time recommended on the packet.

Heat a large, lidded frying pan over medium heat and add the oil, onion, capsicum, garlic and chilli. Fry for about 5 minutes, then add the passata and simmer, covered, for 10 minutes. Carefully transfer to a high-speed blender, add the parmesan cheese and blend to a smooth purée, adding the butter a few cubes at a time to emulsify into the sauce.

Return the frying pan to the heat and add the pasta and sauce along with about ¼ cup (60 ml/2 fl oz) of the pasta water and mix until the sauce thickens and coats the pasta. Transfer to a serving plate and drizzle with plenty of the smoked paprika oil.

Tip

Don't skip the smoked paprika oil. Flavoured oils are one of the easiest ways to add flavour to a meal and you could use this for all kinds of things, from drizzling over barbecued prawns (shrimp) to adding an accent to a salad.

SERVES 4–6

Active time
10 minutes

Cooking time
15 minutes

PACCHERI WITH PANCETTA AND PISTACHIO

One of the easiest ways to make a pasta meal feel fancier is to use a different variety of pasta. Paccheri is a little like extra-fat rigatoni and it's one of my favourites at the moment. The addition of pistachios makes this dish fancier still.

500 g (1 lb 2 oz) giant paccheri

¼ cup (60 ml/2 fl oz) olive oil

250 g (9 oz) pancetta

1 small onion, finely chopped

4 garlic cloves, finely chopped

150 ml (5 fl oz) thickened (whipping) cream

½ cup (50 g/1¾ oz) freshly grated parmesan cheese, plus extra to serve

½ cup (60 g/2 oz) crushed pistachio nuts, to serve

black pepper, to serve

Bring a large saucepan of salted water to the boil. Cook the pasta according to the packet directions, but start checking it about 2 minutes before the end of the recommended cooking time.

Heat a large frying pan over medium heat and add the oil and pancetta. Fry for about 2 minutes until the pancetta is crisp, then remove from the pan with a slotted spoon and set aside. Add the onion and garlic to the oil in the pan. Cook for about 6 minutes then add the cream and parmesan and bring to a simmer.

Add the pasta and about ½ cup (125 ml/4 fl oz) of the pasta water, then add the reserved pancetta and toss together until the mixture creates a creamy sauce. Scatter with crushed pistachios, extra parmesan and black pepper to serve.

Tip

You want to add enough of the pasta water so that the 'sauce' looks a little watery as it comes off the heat. About the texture of pouring cream is right, so that as it cools the sauce thickens to the consistency of thickened cream and coats the pasta.

SPAGHETTI VONGOLE ROSSO

SERVES 4–6

Active time
5 minutes

Cooking time
15 minutes

Vongole has been one of my favourite pastas ever since I tried it as a 17-year-old visiting Italy for the first time. I was in a touristy cafe in the touristy town of Burano near Venice, but as I sat outside eating my plate of spaghetti with my family the only thought in my head was, 'How can life get any better than this?'

600 g (1 lb 5 oz) pipis or clams (vongole)

½ cup (125 ml/4 fl oz) olive oil

5 garlic cloves, sliced

½ teaspoon chilli flakes

1 cup (250 ml/8½ fl oz) white wine

¾ cup (180 ml/6 fl oz) tomato passata (puréed tomatoes)

1 cup (160 g/5½ oz) cherry tomatoes

1 teaspoon fish sauce (optional)

500 g (1 lb 2 oz) spaghetti

½ cup (30 g/1 oz) finely shredded parsley

Bring a large saucepan of salted water to the boil. Cook the pasta according to the packet directions, but start checking it about 2 minutes before the end of the recommended cooking time.

Heat a large frying pan (big enough to hold the pipis and the pasta) over medium heat. Add the oil and garlic and fry for about a minute until the garlic starts to brown around the edges, then add the chilli and white wine. Cover and simmer for a minute, then add the passata, cherry tomatoes and fish sauce, if using.

Simmer the tomatoes for 3–5 minutes until they start to burst. Add the pipis, cover and shake the pan. Cook for about 3 minutes until about half of them are opened. At this point the spaghetti should be about two-thirds cooked. Transfer it to the pipis with about 1 cup (250 ml/ 8½ fl oz) of the pasta water. Stir the spaghetti through the pipis until the spaghetti is al dente and the pipis are all opened. Stir through the parsley and serve.

Tip

Remove about half of the shells of the vongole before serving. It only takes a few seconds but makes for a prettier dish as well as making it easier to eat.

SERVES 4–6

Active time
10 minutes

Cooking time
15 minutes

CHICKEN AND CREAM CHEESE PENNE

Pasta is an affordable dinner not just because the pasta itself is cheap, but because you don't need many other ingredients to flavour it. In this dish, just a little bit of chicken goes a very long way.

500 g (1 lb 2 oz) penne

300 g (10½ oz) chicken breast, cut into 2 cm (¾ in) cubes

salt and black pepper, to season, plus extra to serve

3 tablespoons olive oil

1 small onion, finely diced

4 garlic cloves, minced

150 g (5½ oz) cream cheese

2 cups (260 g/9 oz) frozen baby peas

1 teaspoon dried oregano

Bring a large saucepan of salted water to the boil. Cook the pasta according to the packet directions, but start checking it about 2 minutes before the end of the recommended cooking time.

Season the chicken with salt and pepper. Heat a very large frying pan over medium heat. Add the oil, onion and garlic and fry for about 2 minutes until the onion is fragrant and softened, but not browned. Add the chicken and cook for about 3 minutes until it is about three-quarters of the way cooked. Add the cream cheese, peas and oregano and stir until the cream cheese is melted.

When the pasta is al dente, transfer it to the pan with about ½ cup (125 ml/4 fl oz) of the pasta water. Toss everything together to create a smooth sauce that is thick enough to coat the pasta. Serve with plenty of black pepper.

Tip

As I mentioned at the beginning of this chapter, the emulsification of the oils in the pasta (in this case, olive oil and the oils from the cream cheese) with the pasta water is all-important. I'll even use a little bit of starch slurry to help this along, just like I do when stir-frying.

TINNED FISH WITH CAPERS AND TOMATO SPAGHETTI

SERVES 4–6

Active time
10 minutes

Cooking time
15 minutes

There's nothing wrong with tuna, but there are so many other varieties of tinned seafood to explore. The tomato pasta here is just a base for showcasing some interesting fish.

½ cup (125 ml/4 fl oz) olive oil

1 onion, diced

3 garlic cloves, roughly chopped

1 tablespoon baby capers

2 cups (500 ml/17 fl oz) tomato passata (puréed tomatoes)

salt and pepper, to season

500 g (1 lb 2 oz) spaghetti

190 g (6½ oz) good-quality tinned fish (e.g. smoked tuna, mackerel, etc.)

Heat a large, lidded frying pan over medium heat. Add the oil, onion and garlic and cook for about 5 minutes until softened. Add the capers and passata, season with salt and pepper and simmer for 10 minutes.

Bring a large saucepan of salted water to the boil. Cook the pasta according to the packet directions, but start checking it about 2 minutes before the end of the recommended cooking time.

Add the pasta to the cooked sauce along with about ¼ cup (60 ml/2 fl oz) of the pasta water and mix well. Remove to a serving plate and serve with the tinned fish.

Tip

Try mackerel, clams, trout, smoked oysters or just about any other tinned fish you can think of with this dish. It's worth keeping a few favourites in your pantry.

LINGUINE WITH MUSSELS AND PANCETTA

SERVES 4–6

Active time
10 minutes

Cooking time
15 minutes

Overcooked mussels are rubbery, dry and lacking flavour. The best advice I've ever received about cooking mussels was from a mussel farmer who told me to just remove the mussels one by one from the pot as they open, whether boiling or steaming. No more overcooked mussels.

500 g (1 lb 2 oz) linguine

1 kg (2 lb 3 oz) mussels, cleaned and debearded (see Tip, below)

¼ cup (60 ml/2 fl oz) olive oil, plus extra

150 g (5½ oz) pancetta, cut into lardons

½ small onion, finely diced

3 garlic cloves, sliced

½ cup (125 ml/4 fl oz) white wine

salt and pepper, to season

150 ml (5 fl oz) thickened (whipping) cream

2 tablespoons finely shredded parsley, to serve

Bring a large saucepan of salted water to the boil. Cook the pasta according to the packet directions, but start checking it about 2 minutes before the end of the recommended cooking time.

Place a large frying pan over high heat and add about 1 cup (250 ml/ 8½ fl oz) water. Add the mussels and cook for about 3 minutes, removing the individual mussels as soon as they open. Remove the mussels from their shells. Strain the liquid and set both the mussels and liquid aside. Rinse out the pan to remove any grit released by the mussels.

Return the pan to medium heat and add the olive oil and pancetta. Fry until the pancetta is crisp, then remove from the pan and set aside. Add the onion and garlic to the pan and cook for about 2 minutes until softened. Add the wine and cook for further 2 minutes until the wine stops smelling alcoholic. Add about ½ cup (125 ml/4 fl oz) of the mussel liquid and the cream and bring to a simmer.

When the pasta is al dente, add it to the sauce and stir until it has absorbed most of the sauce. Stir through the mussels, pancetta and parsley and serve.

Tip

Most farmed mussels come pot-ready: cleaned, debearded and ready to cook so you don't need to do anything to them. That said, if you do have mussels or clams that need purging, mix together 30 g of salt for every 4 cups (1 litre/34 fl oz) water and soak the mussels in the salt solution for 30 minutes.

SERVES 4–6

Active time
5 minutes

Cooking time
10 minutes

PASTA ALLA CARLOFORTINA

San Pietro is a small tuna-fishing island off Sardinia that was settled by migrants from Liguria in the eighteenth century. This dish is named after the main town on the island, Carloforte, and combines Ligurian pesto with the island's famous tuna. That's a lot of history for a dish that you can make in 10 minutes out of ingredients from your pantry.

500 g (1 lb 2 oz) casarecce

½ cup (125 ml/4 fl oz) olive oil

250 g (9 oz) mixed cherry tomatoes, halved

190 g (6½ oz) tinned tuna chunks in spring water

200 g (7 oz) basil pesto

Bring a large saucepan of salted water to the boil. Cook the pasta according to the packet directions, but start checking it about 2 minutes before the end of the recommended cooking time.

Place a large frying pan over high heat and add the oil and the cherry tomatoes. Cook until the tomatoes start to soften, then break the tuna into the pan in large chunks.

When the pasta is al dente, add it to the pan along with the pesto and about ¼ cup (60 ml/2 fl oz) of the pasta water. Toss the pasta until it's coated with the sauce and serve.

Tip

This is more often made with trofie instead of casarecce, just like a classic Genoan-style pesto pasta, but I've suggested casarecce as its texture is similar and it's far more readily available.

SERVES 4–6

Active time
5 minutes

Cooking time
10 minutes

'ANTIPASTA'

Smart cooking is quick cooking. This quick pasta is about taking advantage of the time someone else has put into drying tomatoes, marinating vegetables and brining olives, and using those flavours to enhance a simple plate of spaghetti.

500 g (1 lb 2 oz) spaghetti

1 cup (125 g/4½ oz) mixed antipasto, e.g. sun-dried tomatoes, marinated artichokes, marinated eggplant (aubergine), marinated capsicum (bell pepper)

½ cup (125 ml/4 fl oz) olive oil

2 garlic cloves, thinly sliced

1 bird's eye chilli, sliced

1 cup (125 g/4½ oz) mixed marinated olives, pitted and halved

1 cup (150 g/5½ oz) cherry bocconcini (fresh baby mozzarella), drained and halved

freshly grated parmesan cheese, to serve

black pepper, to serve

Bring a large saucepan of salted water to the boil. Cook the pasta according to the packet directions, but start checking it about 2 minutes before the end of the recommended cooking time.

Cut the antipasto into bite-sized pieces. Heat a large frying pan over medium heat and add the oil, garlic and chilli. Fry for about 2 minutes until the garlic just starts to brown around the edges. Add the antipasto and olives and stir.

When the pasta is al dente, add it to the pan with about ¼ cup (60 ml/2 fl oz) of the pasta water and toss to coat the pasta in the oil and sauce. Stir through the bocconcini and allow it to melt just a little. Serve with a little grated parmesan and black pepper.

Tip

Many of these marinated products will be shelf stable, so save yourself some shopping time by keeping a few jars of marinated vegetables in your pantry ready for a dish like this, or simply for serving as antipasto if you don't feel like pasta.

SERVES 4–6

Active time
10 minutes

Cooking time
10 minutes

PANTRY PASTA

Pasta is made for pantry dinners. This recipe is based on two tins – one of tomatoes and one of evaporated milk – and the result is very similar to the popular pasta alla vodka. The vodka in that dish is used to add umami. I've used a bit of stock powder here for that same purpose, but you could use vodka instead if you liked.

500 g (1 lb 2 oz) mafaldine

¼ cup (60 ml/2 fl oz) olive oil

2 garlic cloves, thinly sliced

400 g (14½ oz) tinned chopped tomatoes

1 teaspoon vegetable stock powder

½ teaspoon chilli flakes

300 ml (10 fl oz) evaporated milk

freshly grated parmesan cheese, to serve (optional)

black pepper, to serve

Bring a large saucepan of salted water to the boil. Cook the pasta according to the packet directions, but start checking it about 2 minutes before the end of the recommended cooking time.

Heat a large frying pan over medium heat and add the oil and garlic. Fry for about 2 minutes until the garlic just starts to brown around the edges. Add the tomatoes, stock powder and chilli flakes, cover and simmer for about 5 minutes. Add the evaporated milk and mix well.

When the pasta is al dente, add it to the pan with about ½ cup (125 ml/4 fl oz) of the pasta water and toss to coat the pasta in the sauce. Serve with a little grated parmesan and black pepper.

Tip

I like mafaldine for this because it is an interesting pasta shape – almost like a long version of a short pasta. When your pasta sauce is very simple, a more unusual pasta shape can make your meal feel a little more special.

CREAMY LEMON PASTA

SERVES 4–6

Active time
5 minutes

Cooking time
15 minutes

Don't be fooled – creamy pastas don't need a lot of cream! The creamy texture of the sauce is more about the emulsification of the pasta water with the fats used in the dish. I've used evaporated milk here as it's a great pantry product and lower in saturated fat than cream.

500 g (1 lb 2 oz) bucatini or other long pasta

1 cup (250 ml/8½ fl oz) evaporated milk

juice and zest of 1 lemon

½ teaspoon vegetable stock powder

50 g (1¾ oz) butter

1 cup (100 g/3½ oz) grated parmesan cheese, plus extra to serve

black pepper, to serve

Bring a large saucepan of salted water to the boil. Cook the pasta according to the packet directions, but start checking it about 2 minutes before the end of the recommended cooking time.

Heat a large frying pan over medium heat and add the evaporated milk, lemon zest and stock powder. Bring to a simmer, then whisk in the butter and parmesan to form a smooth sauce. Add the pasta and lemon juice, and about ½ cup (125 ml/4 fl oz) of the pasta water and mix until the sauce is thickened to the consistency of pouring cream.

Serve with a little extra grated parmesan and black pepper.

Tip

Don't be shy with your pasta water. I've put ½ cup (125 ml/4 fl oz) in the recipe but depending on your pasta you may need to add more to create a creamy sauce.

QUICK WOKS

THE WOK IS THE UNDISPUTED HERO OF QUICK COOKING, AND I TRULY COULD NOT LIVE WITHOUT IT.

I can't tell you the number of times my response to the evening dinner panic has been to take whatever I have on hand and stir-fry it – be it eggs, a few frozen prawns, quite literally any vegetable I might have in the crisper, or any little bit of meat or seafood I might have lying around. No matter what you have, you can turn it into a dish.

The true genius of the wok is that it allows you to combine meats and vegetables in just about any proportion and season them as simply as possible. In my wok cooking, I almost always use something salty and umami-packed (e.g. salt and Shaoxing wine, a bit of soy sauce or oyster sauce, concentrated chicken stock) and then balance it with a touch of sugar. It really is that simple.

In this chapter, most of the recipes are just two or three main ingredients, the seasonings above, and aromatics (choose your own adventure from the holy trinity of Chinese cooking – garlic, ginger and onion).

The challenge is understanding your wok. The good news is I've taught LOTS of people to cook with woks and none closer to home than my wife, Asami. She'd be the first to admit that her stir-fried dishes never really turned out all that well when she first started using a wok. Now she's a pro. These are her three golden tips:

1. Heat the wok first and use more oil than you think you will need.
2. Don't put too much into the wok at one time.
3. Adjust the texture with starch solution at the end.

Let's talk about all of them. First, I am a big proponent of vegetable oils in cooking. They have a high proportion of monounsaturated fats, just like olive oil, and in wok cooking and you need to use enough oil to ensure your wok performs properly. Don't be scared of the oil! For the past 60 years, the fear of fat has had a stranglehold on how we think about food in Australia.

There's a big difference between saturated fats and unsaturated fats when it comes to health. Traditional Mediterranean and Asian diets commonly include unsaturated fats from oils like olive, sunflower, canola, etc. These should not be considered the same as saturated fats from butter or lard.

Second, putting too much into a wok is one of the cardinal sins of wok cooking. If you fill your wok with ingredients, they'll stew more than stir-fry. We often envision stir-fried dishes as a whole riot of different vegetables, but most stir-fries that I make are just two main ingredients, and I usually make a portion big enough for one or two plates. Any more than that and I'll fry each individual ingredient separately before mixing everything together at the end.

The last tip is a very underrated step in wok cooking: adjust the texture with a mixture of starch (usually cornflour/cornstarch or potato starch) and cold water at the end of cooking. It's essential to get the texture right. As ingredients in a wok cook, they release their own liquid – basically a stock – and that liquid, together with any liquid seasonings you might add, can be thickened to a sauce to coat the ingredients. Think of it like any other sauce: too thin and your stir-fry will be insipid, too thick and your stir-fry will be gluggy.

Just like the addition of pasta water to a pasta dish, or whisking chilled butter into a French sauce, tossing your wok-fried dish with a little starch mixture will emulsify your cooking oil with the juices from the ingredients, creating a luxurious sauce that is the key to a great-tasting wok dish.

171	**PRAWNS AND EGGS**
172	**SHANGHAI SHREDDED PORK AND CABBAGE**
175	**THREE-CUP CHICKEN**
177	**BEEF PAD PRIK KHING**
178	**CHICKEN AND SNOW PEAS WITH OYSTER SAUCE**
181	**SEAFOOD YAKISOBA**
183	**CHICKEN AND CHOY SUM**
184	**FRIED EGGS AND SOY SAUCE**
187	**BEEF, ASPARAGUS AND CAPSICUM**
189	**STIR-FRIED PORK AND FENNEL**
190	**BEEF PAD SEE EW**

PRAWNS AND EGGS

MAKES 1 DISH FOR A SHARED MEAL

Active time
5 minutes

Cooking time
5 minutes

I always have frozen prawns (shrimp) in the freezer and eggs in the fridge, so this is one dish I know I can make at a moment's notice.

5 eggs, beaten

white pepper, to season

½ teaspoon sesame oil

½ teaspoon cornflour (cornstarch) or potato starch mixed with 2 tablespoons cold water

a good pinch of MSG or chicken stock powder

⅓ cup (80 ml/2½ fl oz) vegetable oil

200 g (7 oz) prawn (shrimp) meat, thawed, deveined and butterflied (see Tip, below)

salt, to season

2 thin spring onions (scallions), finely sliced

Whisk together the eggs, pepper, sesame oil, starch mixture and MSG or stock powder. Heat a wok over high heat and add 1 tablespoon of vegetable oil. Add the prawns, season with salt and fry for 2 minutes until the prawns are nearly cooked through, then remove from the wok.

Return the wok to the heat and add the remaining oil. Add the egg mixture. Mix well, then, when the heat starts to set the eggs, slowly push the egg away from the edges of the wok to the centre to scramble it. Season with salt. When the egg is nearly completely set, return the prawns to the wok and mix gently. Remove to a serving plate and scatter with spring onions to serve.

Tip

I always butterfly prawns by splitting them almost the entire way through along the length of the back. As they cook they curl in two directions for a fantastic texture in your dish.

MAKES 1 DISH FOR A SHARED MEAL

Active time
5 minutes

Cooking time
5 minutes

SHANGHAI SHREDDED PORK AND CABBAGE

A simple dish like this is a good model for many stir-fries. Just a couple of main ingredients (in this case, pork and cabbage), seasoned simply.

250 g (9 oz) pork shoulder, very thinly sliced

¼ Chinese cabbage (wombok), thinly sliced

2 tablespoons vegetable oil

1 cm (½ in) fresh ginger, thinly sliced

2 garlic cloves, thinly sliced

salt, to season

1 tablespoon concentrated liquid chicken stock or 1 teaspoon chicken stock powder

1 tablespoon Shaoxing wine

1 teaspoon sugar

¼ teaspoon ground white pepper

1 teaspoon cornflour (cornstarch) or potato starch mixed with ¼ cup (60 ml/2 fl oz) cold water

steamed rice, to serve

MARINADE

½ teaspoon cornflour (cornstarch) or potato starch

½ teaspoon salt, plus extra to season

½ teaspoon concentrated liquid chicken stock or ¼ teaspoon chicken stock powder

½ teaspoon bicarbonate of soda (baking soda)

1 teaspoon vegetable oil

Combine the pork with the marinade ingredients and set aside. Place the Chinese cabbage in a large heatproof bowl and pour over boiling water. Stand for just a minute, then drain.

Heat a wok over high heat. Add the oil, and fry the pork until it separates. Add the ginger and garlic and fry until fragrant. Add the cabbage and season with salt, chicken stock powder, Shaoxing wine, sugar and white pepper. Toss until the cabbage is wilted, then thicken the juices with the starch mixture. Transfer to a serving plate and serve with rice.

Tip

Chicken stock is one of my main stir-fry seasonings. You can use homemade liquid stock, but powder or concentrated liquid stock (both available from Asian grocers) are much better for stir-frying because they contain less liquid.

SERVES 4

Active time
10 minutes

Cooking time
10 minutes

THREE-CUP CHICKEN

This Taiwanese classic gets its name from the three seasonings – soy sauce, wine and sesame oil. Many recipes call for the three seasonings to be added in the same measure, but I think it's better this way.

2 tablespoons vegetable oil

2 cm (¾ in) ginger, thickly sliced

8 garlic cloves, bruised

600 g (1 lb 5 oz) boneless chicken thighs, cut into 3 cm (1¼ in) pieces

3 tablespoons sake or Shaoxing wine

1 tablespoon soy sauce

1 tablespoon dark soy sauce

1 tablespoon sugar

2 teaspoons sesame oil

1 large red chilli, sliced on an angle

2 cups (60 g/2 oz) loosely packed Thai basil

Heat a wok over high heat and add the vegetable oil. Add the ginger and garlic and fry for about 2 minutes until the garlic is starting to brown. Add the chicken and fry until lightly browned. Add the wine, soy sauces and sugar and bring to a simmer. Simmer for about 5 minutes until the chicken is cooked through and the sauce is reduced enough to coat the chicken, then stir through the chilli and basil and serve.

Tip

I don't bother peeling ginger for stir-fried dishes when I'm adding it as a thick slice. You can even pick it out. This is home cooking not a fancy restaurant. Just eat around it.

BEEF PAD PRIK KHING

MAKES 1 DISH FOR A SHARED MEAL

Active time
10 minutes

Cooking time
10 minutes

Beef is simply stir-fried with red curry paste and beans for a flavourful dish that can be ready from start to finish in about 10 minutes. Find a brand of curry paste that you like and stick with it. Using the same brand of paste means you'll already have a good idea how to season any dishes you use it in.

- 200 g (7 oz) flank or rump steak or topside, thinly sliced
- 3 tablespoons vegetable oil, plus extra if needed
- 1½ tablespoons red curry paste
- 3 makrut lime leaves, torn
- 2 garlic cloves, roughly chopped
- 250 g (9 oz) green beans, tailed and cut into 5 cm (2 in) lengths
- 1 large red chilli, sliced
- 2 teaspoons sugar
- 1 teaspoon fish sauce (optional; see Tip, below)
- a squeeze of lemon or lime juice, to serve

MARINADE

- 1 teaspoon soy sauce
- ¼ teaspoon bicarbonate of soda (baking soda)
- 1 teaspoon cornflour (cornstarch) or potato starch
- 1 teaspoon vegetable oil

Combine the meat with the marinade ingredients and set aside.

Heat a wok over high heat and add the oil. Add the beef and spread it out in a single layer over the base of the wok. Fry for about 3 minutes, without stirring, until the beef is well browned on one side. Toss and cook for a further minute. Remove from the wok.

Add a little more oil if needed, then add the curry paste and lime leaves and fry until the paste is fragrant. Add the garlic, beans and chilli and toss until the beans are softened. Return the meat to the wok and season with sugar (and fish sauce, if needed) and add a little water to moisten if necessary. Transfer to a serving plate, squeeze over a little lemon or lime juice and serve.

Tip

Commercial curry pastes are usually heavily seasoned so it's unlikely that you'll need to use fish sauce for this recipe, though if you are using homemade curry pastes then it might be a good idea. The squeeze of citrus isn't traditional, but I find it very helpful when using commercial pastes because they lack sourness.

CHICKEN AND SNOW PEAS WITH OYSTER SAUCE

MAKES 1 DISH FOR A SHARED MEAL

Active time
10 minutes

Cooking time
5 minutes

A simple chicken stir-fry is a mid-week lifesaver. This one is with snow peas (mange tout), but you could easily substitute those for celery, mushrooms, Asian greens, capsicum (bell pepper) or any other vegetable you can think of.

250 g (9 oz) boneless chicken thighs, thinly sliced

2 tablespoons vegetable oil

½ onion, thickly sliced

2 garlic cloves, sliced

1 cm (½ in) ginger, sliced

250 g (9 oz) snow peas (mange tout), tailed and sliced in half on a diagonal

2 teaspoons soy sauce

1 teaspoon Shaoxing wine

1 tablespoon oyster sauce

¼ teaspoon sugar

1 teaspoon cornflour (cornstarch) or potato starch mixed with ¼ cup (60 ml/2 fl oz) cold water

MARINADE

1 teaspoon soy sauce

¼ teaspoon bicarbonate of soda (baking soda)

1 teaspoon Shaoxing wine

½ teaspoon cornflour (cornstarch) or potato starch

1 teaspoon vegetable oil

Combine the chicken with the marinade ingredients and set aside.

Heat a wok over high heat and add the oil. Add the chicken and spread it out in a single layer over the base of the wok. Fry for about 2 minutes without stirring until the chicken starts to brown.

Add the onion, garlic and ginger and toss the chicken and fry for a further minute. Add the snow peas, soy sauce, wine, oyster sauce and sugar. Toss until the snow peas are just tender. If the wok is too dry, add a few tablespoons of water (or stock), then add as much of the cornflour mixture as you need to produce a silky sauce and serve.

Tip

Adding a little bicarbonate of soda to your marinades lowers the pH and reduces the strength of protein bonds that form as the meat cooks and tightens so it remains more tender. It only takes a few minutes of marinating to have a noticeable effect.

SEAFOOD YAKISOBA

SERVES 4

Active time
10 minutes

Cooking time
15 minutes

Noodle dishes, like pasta, should be mainly about the noodles. Don't try to overload them too much with extra ingredients, and instead really concentrate on getting the texture and taste of the noodles themselves right.

¼ cup (60 ml/2 fl oz) vegetable oil

1 cup (75 g/2¾ oz) cabbage, cut into 5 cm (2 in) pieces

1 small carrot, cut into matchsticks

1 small onion, thickly sliced

4 fresh shiitake mushrooms, thinly sliced

250 g (9 oz) good-quality seafood marinara mix

2 packets (approx. 500 g/1 lb 2 oz) yakisoba noodles (thin, yellow Japanese noodles)

1 handful of bonito flakes

1 tablespoon benishouga (red julienned pickled ginger), to serve

aonori (Japanese green sea lettuce flakes), to serve

Japanese mayonnaise, to serve

 YAKISOBA SAUCE

2 tablespoons oyster sauce

2 tablespoons Worcestershire sauce

2 tablespoons tomato sauce (ketchup)

2 tablespoons dark soy sauce

1 teaspoon sugar

To make the yakisoba sauce, combine the ingredients together and stir to dissolve the sugar.

Heat a very large frying pan, barbecue hotplate or wok over high heat. Add about 1 tablespoon of the vegetable oil and fry the vegetables until softened and lightly browned in places. Remove from the pan. Add another tablespoon of the oil and fry the marinara mix until almost cooked through, then remove from the pan.

Microwave the noodles for a minute to separate them, then add the remaining oil and fry the noodles until lightly toasted and separated. Add the vegetables and as much of the sauce as you like, and toss to combine. Stir through the seafood, bonito flakes and benishouga and remove to a plate. Scatter with the aonori and serve with mayonnaise.

Tip

Good-quality marinara mix is a lifesaver. Find a good fishmonger and you'll find a good marinara mix.

CHICKEN AND CHOY SUM

MAKES 1 DISH FOR A SHARED MEAL

Active time
5 minutes

Cooking time
5 minutes

You guessed it: another stir-fry of just two main ingredients – in this case, chicken and choy sum. While some stir-fries in this book show you how to change up the meat and vegetables, this recipe shows how you can change up the seasonings, too.

250 g (9 oz) boneless chicken thighs, thinly sliced

3 tablespoons vegetable oil

2 garlic cloves, roughly chopped

3 dried red chillies, broken into pieces

1 bunch choy sum, cut into 2 cm (¾ in) lengths

1 tablespoon Shaoxing wine

2 tablespoons Chinese olive vegetable (see Tip, below)

½ teaspoon sugar

½ teaspoon cornflour (cornstarch) or potato starch mixed with ¼ cup (60 ml/2 fl oz) cold water

MARINADE

1 teaspoon soy sauce

¼ teaspoon bicarbonate of soda (baking soda)

1 teaspoon Shaoxing wine

½ teaspoon cornflour (cornstarch) or potato starch

1 teaspoon vegetable oil

Combine the chicken with the marinade ingredients and set aside.

Heat a wok over high heat and add the oil. Add the chicken and spread it out in a single layer over the base of the wok. Fry for about 2 minutes without stirring until the chicken starts to brown. Toss and fry for a further minute. Remove the chicken from the wok leaving the oil in the wok.

Add the garlic and chilli and fry for a minute until fragrant. Add the choy sum and cook, tossing, for 1–2 minutes. Return the chicken to the wok and add the Shaoxing wine, Chinese olive vegetable (or oyster sauce) and sugar and toss until well mixed. Drizzle in a little cornflour mixture and toss to thicken, then serve.

Tip

Chinese olive vegetable is a savoury jarred preparation available from Asian grocers. It's a mixture of pickled *Canarium album* fruit and mustard greens. You could use pickled mustard greens, black beans or simply oyster sauce as a substitute.

**MAKES 1 DISH FOR
A SHARED MEAL**

Active time
5 minutes

Cooking time
10 minutes

FRIED EGGS AND SOY SAUCE

Growing up, most of my meals were Chinese, and each night the table would be a mixture of new dishes and ones that were left over from the days before. If the table ever needed just a little something extra, there would be a simple dish of a few fried eggs topped with soy sauce. You could use ordinary soy sauce but I've given you a very versatile sweet version you can keep in your fridge.

6 eggs

1 teaspoon sesame oil

¼ teaspoon MSG or stock powder

2–3 tablespoons vegetable oil

1 spring onion (scallion), thinly sliced, to serve

white pepper, to season

 CANTONESE SWEET SOY SAUCE

1 tablespoon vegetable oil

2 spring onions (scallions), cut into 5 cm (2 in) lengths

2 garlic cloves, bruised

2 cm (¾ in) ginger, sliced

½ cup (125 ml/4 fl oz) soy sauce

2 tablespoons dark soy sauce

2 tablespoons sugar

To make the Cantonese sweet soy sauce, heat a small saucepan over medium heat. Add the oil, spring onion, garlic and ginger. Fry for about 2 minutes until the onion and garlic are starting to brown, then add the soy sauces and sugar plus 2 tablespoons of water. Bring to a simmer and cook for 5 minutes, then strain into a glass jar. The sweet soy sauce will keep in the fridge for months.

Crack the eggs into a large bowl, add the sesame oil and sprinkle over the MSG or stock powder. You don't need to beat the eggs (though you can if you like).

Heat a wok over high heat until very hot and add the oil. Add the eggs and push them with your wok tool a few times until the eggs are just set the way you like them. I like set whites but the yolks a little runny. Some of the yolks will break (maybe all of them) and mix with the whites, but the idea is to get a mixed appearance. Transfer to a serving plate, drizzle with a little of the sweet soy sauce, scatter with spring onions and sprinkle with a little white pepper.

Tip

Make extra of this Cantonese sweet soy sauce. You can use it as a stir-fry sauce or for drizzling over chicken or salmon. It's versatile and delicious.

MAKES 1 DISH FOR A SHARED MEAL

Active time
10 minutes

Cooking time
10 minutes

BEEF, ASPARAGUS AND CAPSICUM

Most recipes will call for you to fry the meat first and the vegetables second, which is how it is usually done in a restaurant to ensure the vegetables remain crisp. For home cooking, however, I think frying the vegetables first makes more sense as you then don't need to rinse the wok after frying the meat.

300 g (10½ oz) topside or rump steak, thinly sliced

⅓ cup (80 ml/2½ fl oz) vegetable oil

1 cm (½ in) fresh ginger, peeled and sliced into thin matchsticks

1 red onion, thickly sliced

1 bunch asparagus, cut into 5 cm (2 in) lengths

1 red capsicum (bell pepper), cut into large chunks

2 garlic cloves, sliced

2 tablespoons oyster sauce

1 tablespoon soy sauce

2 teaspoons Shaoxing wine

1 teaspoon sugar

1 teaspoon cornflour (cornstarch) or potato starch mixed with ¼ cup (60 ml/2 fl oz) cold water

MARINADE

1 teaspoon soy sauce

dash of dark soy sauce

1 teaspoon Shaoxing wine

¼ teaspoon bicarbonate of soda (baking soda)

½ teaspoon cornflour (cornstarch) or potato starch

1 teaspoon vegetable oil

Combine the beef with the marinade ingredients and set aside.

Heat a wok over high heat and add 1 tablespoon of the vegetable oil. Add the ginger, onion, asparagus and capsicum and toss for a minute until slightly softened but still crisp. Remove from the wok, leaving the oil in the base.

Return the wok to heat and add the remaining oil. Add the beef and spread it out in a single layer over the base of the wok. Fry for about 3 minutes without stirring until the beef is well browned on one side. Toss the beef, then add the garlic, and fry for a minute until the garlic is lightly browned. Return the vegetables to the wok. Add the oyster sauce, soy sauce, wine and sugar and toss to combine, then add as much of the starch mixture as you need to produce a silky sauce. Serve.

Tip

The recipes in this chapter suggest either cornflour (cornstarch) or potato starch. They perform very similarly, but with slight differences in their thickening properties both in the wok and after reheating. I mainly use potato starch, but for most purposes they are largely interchangeable.

STIR-FRIED PORK AND FENNEL

MAKES 1 DISH FOR A SHARED MEAL

Active time
10 minutes

Cooking time
10 minutes

I'm not sure why fennel isn't used as a stir-fry ingredient more often. It has a great texture and flavour, and it doesn't release much liquid. In the wok it performs very similarly to celery, another of my favourite stir-fry ingredients.

- 3 tablespoons vegetable oil
- 2 small fennel bulbs (or 1 large one), cut into 1 cm (½ in) wedges
- 2 cm (¾ in) ginger, peeled and thinly sliced
- 3 thick spring onions (scallions), sliced on a sharp diagonal
- 3 large dried red chillies, cut into 2 cm (¾ in) lengths
- 300 g (10½ oz) pork belly, skin and bones removed, sliced
- salt, to season
- 1 tablespoon Shaoxing wine
- 1 tablespoon concentrated liquid chicken stock
- ½ teaspoon sugar
- 1 teaspoon cornflour (cornstarch) or potato starch mixed with ¼ cup (60 ml/2 fl oz) cold water

Heat a wok over high heat and add the oil. Fry the fennel and ginger until lightly browned, then add the spring onion and chilli and toss for a minute. Remove from the wok.

Return the wok to the heat and add the pork belly. Season with salt and fry until well browned on one side. Toss the wok, then return the vegetables to the wok. Add the wine, stock and sugar and toss for a minute, then add as much of the starch mixture as you need to produce a silky sauce. Serve.

Tip

Head to an Asian grocer to find concentrated liquid chicken stock. It's similar to the ones you can buy in small 'pots' at the supermarket, but cheaper and with less packaging. If you can't find the right stock, you can use oyster sauce instead.

BEEF PAD SEE EW

SERVES 4

Active time
5 minutes

Cooking time
15 minutes

Pad see ew is just one of a number of flat rice noodle dishes around South-East Asia, like char kway teow and beef chow fun, that taste best with a bit of wok hei (the breath of a wok) to them. My advice is to heat the noodles (using hot water or a microwave) so they don't suck too much heat from the wok, and only cook one serving at a time.

200 g (7 oz) beef topside, thinly sliced

600 g (1 lb 5 oz) fresh flat, wide rice noodles

½ cup (125 ml/4 fl oz) vegetable oil

4 eggs

1 small bunch gai lan (Chinese broccoli), thinly sliced

6 garlic cloves, roughly chopped

white pepper, to serve

thinly sliced bird's eye chilli, to serve

lemon wedges and extra Golden Mountain sauce (see Tip, below), to serve

MARINADE

¼ teaspoon bicarbonate of soda (baking soda)

½ teaspoon dark soy sauce

1 teaspoon Golden Mountain sauce

1 teaspoon vegetable oil

pinch of sugar

PAD SEE EW SAUCE

2 tablespoons oyster sauce

1 tablespoon soy sauce

2 teaspoons dark soy sauce

2 teaspoons fish sauce

2 teaspoons Golden Mountain sauce

1½ tablespoons sugar

Combine the beef with the marinade ingredients and set aside.

To make the pad see ew sauce, combine the ingredients in a bowl, stirring to dissolve the sugar. If you need to, separate the rice noodles by pouring hot water over them and standing for a minute or two before draining and gently separating them with your hands.

Heat a wok over high heat, add about 2 tablespoons of the oil and fry the beef until just cooked. Remove from the wok and set aside. Rinse out the wok.

Return the wok to high heat and add half the remaining oil. Crack 2 eggs into the oil and mix. Add half the gai lan and one-quarter of the garlic and toss until just softened. Add half the noodles and fry until lightly charred. Add half the beef and sauce to taste and toss to combine. Remove to a serving plate and sprinkle with a little white pepper. Repeat for the remaining ingredients.

Serve with some sliced chillies mixed with lemon juice and Golden Mountain sauce.

Tip

Golden Mountain sauce is a savoury seasoning used in Thai and other South-East Asian cooking. It's similar to Maggi seasoning so you could substitute that instead.

QUICK SWEETS

IT'S ALWAYS NICE TO FINISH A MEAL WITH SOMETHING SWEET. IN THIS CHAPTER I'VE TRIED TO CAPTURE SOME SWEETS THAT FIT THE BILL OF EASY BUT JOYFUL. THINGS YOU CAN LOOK FORWARD TO THAT WON'T TAKE HOURS TO PULL TOGETHER.

Nine times out of ten in my household, dessert is a plate of cut fruit and I wouldn't change that for the world. There's something meditative and soulful about cutting fruit for your family, and it's a joy for me to be able to sit down with my children and share some fruit. Our fruit plate changes daily, and my children's eyes light up when different fruits – lychees, grapes, mangoes or dekopon, just to name a few of their favourites – come into season each year.

I remember when my grandparents and parents cut fruit for me when I was young, and I hope when my children have grown up they will also think back fondly to the times we sat on the sofa as a family with a plate of cut fruit between us.

Variety is the spice of life, however: one time out of ten, dessert is something other than fruit and that's cause to rejoice, too.

When you want something quick and sweet, there are plenty of options that don't involve reaching into the freezer and unwrapping an ice cream. Desserts should be easy but not so easy they feel like a bad habit that you'll regret later. And, after all, dessert exists solely for our pleasure, so there's nothing worse than feeling bad after eating it. That defeats the entire purpose.

196	CHOCOLATE GRANITA
199	WEET-BIX MILLE-FEUILLE
201	SCRAMBLED PANCAKES
202	MASALA CHAI
205	DECAFFOGATO
207	BAKED RICE PUDDING WITH PLUM JAM
208	APRICOT AND SOUR CREAM FOOL
210	SUPER-SOFT CHOCOLATE MUG CAKE
212	TOAST SUNDAE
215	ANYTIME CHOCOLATE AND ALMOND COOKIES

CHOCOLATE GRANITA

SERVES 8

Active time
10 minutes

Freezing time
4 hours

I'm a big fan of cocoa powder. It's all the flavour you get in chocolate without the cocoa butter for texture. This means you can get your chocolate flavour in any texture you like, from cakes to drinks to this light, chocolatey granita.

60 g (2 oz) Dutch-processed (unsweetened) cocoa powder

75 g (2¾ oz) pure icing (confectioners') sugar

1 teaspoon vanilla extract

strawberries, to serve

whipped cream, to serve

Combine the cocoa powder, icing sugar and vanilla in a small saucepan and mix with a whisk to remove any large lumps. Whisk in 2 cups (500 ml/17 fl oz) boiling water, a little at a time, to form a smooth mixture. If the sugar and cocoa are not fully dissolved, place the pot over medium heat and whisk until dissolved. Allow to cool, then transfer to a freezer-proof container and freeze for 4 hours or until solid.

Scrape with a fork to form a granita and serve with the strawberries and whipped cream.

Tip

If you want to make the scraping easier, you can scrape with a fork every hour as the granita freezes.

SERVES 4

Active time
10 minutes

Resting time
30 minutes

WEET-BIX MILLE-FEUILLE

One of my favourite French pastry ingredients is pailleté feuilletine – crumbled pieces of crisp crêpe or wafer used to add a crunchy layer to cakes like entremets and gâteaux opéra. That all sounds very fancy, but it's actually a very similar texture to a good-old Weet-Bix.

4 Weet-Bix

1 tablespoon strawberry jam

1 tablespoon melted butter

1 cup (150 g/5½ oz) mixed berries

VANILLA CREAM

300 ml (10 fl oz) thickened (whipping) cream

50 g (1¾ oz) icing (confectioners') sugar, plus extra for dusting

½ teaspoon vanilla extract

To make the vanilla cream, whip the cream together with the icing sugar and vanilla to soft peaks. Transfer to a piping (icing) bag fitted with a petal nozzle and refrigerate for at least 30 minutes.

Split each Weet-Bix in half horizontally to create a thin wafer. Combine the strawberry jam and melted butter and brush over the top of each wafer. Pipe the top of half the wafers with cream and stud with a few berries. Place an extra wafer on top and pipe with cream again. Stud with a few more berries and dust with icing sugar to serve.

Tip

If you don't have a piping bag (or can't be bothered) just crumble the Weet-Bix over a small bowl of cream and berries.

SERVES 4–6

Active time
10 minutes

Cooking time
10 minutes

SCRAMBLED PANCAKES
Kaiserschmarrn

One thing I love about dessert is the way it can hold a special place in our lives. I have a couple of friends who ordered this classic Austrian dessert to share on their first date. They've now been married for many years and they still order it every time they see it on a menu.

4 eggs, separated

1 tablespoon caster (superfine) sugar, plus 2 teaspoons extra for frying

1 teaspoon vanilla extract

200 ml (7 fl oz) milk

1 cup (150 g/5½ oz) plain (all-purpose) flour

1 teaspoon baking powder

a good pinch of salt

25 g (1 oz) butter, plus 10 g (¼ oz) extra for frying

icing (confectioners') sugar, for dusting

jam or apple sauce, to serve

sour cream or whipped cream, to serve

Whisk the egg whites to stiff peaks and set aside. In a separate bowl, whisk together the egg yolks, caster sugar and vanilla, then whisk in the milk, flour and baking powder, a little at a time. Fold in the egg whites and a good pinch of salt.

Heat a large frying pan over medium heat and add the butter. When the butter is melted, pour in the batter and reduce the heat to medium–low. If you have a lid, use it to cover the pancake. Cook for about 6 minutes until the base of the pancake is browned, then cut into quarters with your spatula and flip each quarter to brown the other side. Cook for a few more minutes, then cut up the pancake with your spatula, scrambling the pieces together. Move the pancake pieces to one side of the pan and add the extra caster sugar and butter for frying, allowing it caramelise a little before rolling the pancakes through the sugar mixture.

Dust the pancakes liberally with icing sugar, and serve with the jam and sour cream.

Tip

Rather than apple sauce or jam, you could also serve this with fresh fruit, lashings of maple syrup or ice cream. Or just about any other pancake toppings you enjoy.

SERVES 4

Active time
5 minutes

Cooking time
10 minutes

MASALA CHAI

Sometimes the sweetness you might crave following a meal doesn't need to be a dessert at all. The aroma of a good masala chai is a lovely way to finish.

1 cinnamon stick

4 whole cloves

4 green cardamom pods

4 black peppercorns

1 cm (½ in) fresh ginger, peeled

2 tablespoons loose-leaf black tea (or 5 tea bags)

1 tablespoon sugar

1 cup (250 ml/8½ fl oz) milk

Combine the spices and ginger in a bowl, or mortar and pestle, and pound lightly to break them up a little. Place in a saucepan over medium heat with 2 cups (500 ml/17 fl oz) water and the tea, and bring to a simmer. Simmer for 3 minutes, then add the sugar and milk and simmer for another 3 minutes until thickened and slightly reduced. Strain the tea into a jug or another saucepan and aerate the mixture with a stick blender for a few seconds (see Tip, below). Pour into tea cups to serve.

Tip

Aerating the chai can create a pleasant froth and lighter texture in the drink. Hold the stick blender just at the surface of the liquid so that it pulls air into it to create bubbles. If you don't have a stick blender you can pour or 'pull' the chai between two cups.

DECAFFOGATO

SERVES 1

Active time
5 minutes

Freezing time
30 minutes

I love the idea of an affogato, but a caffeinated coffee after an evening meal would have me sitting bolt upright in bed until the wee hours. Thus, the decaffogato was born.

2 scoops vanilla ice cream

20 ml (¾ fl oz) amaretto, Frangelico or other liqueur (optional)

dark chocolate block, for grating and to serve

1 shot (30 ml/1 fl oz) decaffeinated espresso

salted cashews, to serve (optional)

Place the ice cream in a serving cup and place the cup in the freezer for about 30 minutes. When ready to serve, pour the Frangelico over the ice cream and grate over a little chocolate. Serve with a shot of decaffeinated espresso, and a few cashews, if using, and pieces of dark chocolate on the side.

Tip

The coffee for an affogato doesn't need to be piping hot straight from the machine. I actually prefer to let it sit for a bit to come closer to room temperature so that it doesn't melt the ice cream too quickly.

BAKED RICE PUDDING WITH PLUM JAM

SERVES 6

Active time
5 minutes

Cooking time
1 hour 45 minutes

Resting time
15 minutes

The great thing about this rice pudding is that it's another all-in-one recipe. Just put all the ingredients into a baking dish and bake!

1 cup (220 g/8 oz) arborio rice

80 g (2¾ oz) caster (superfine) sugar

1 vanilla bean, split lengthways and seeds scraped

3 cups (750 ml/25½ fl oz) milk

300 ml (10 fl oz) thickened (whipping) cream

plum jam, to serve

Heat your oven to 140°C (285°F) fan-forced. Combine the rice, sugar, vanilla seeds, milk and cream in a 1.5 litre (51 fl oz) baking dish and stir to combine. Bake, uncovered, for 90 minutes, then switch to the grill setting and grill for a further 15 minutes until a golden crust forms on top. Remove from the oven and stand for 15 minutes.

Scoop the pudding into individual serving bowls and serve with plum jam.

Tip

Risotto rices like arborio or carnaroli are great for this, but I also often use koshihikari (sushi) rice or other short-grain rices. You could also use a long-grain rice like jasmine if you like.

APRICOT AND SOUR CREAM FOOL

SERVES 6

Active time
5 minutes

Cooking time
30 minutes

I love the combination of apricot and pistachio, but it's the vanilla and almond extracts in the cream that give this dish the 'ooh, that's good' X-factor.

300 g (10½ oz) dried apricots, roughly chopped

a good pinch of saffron

60 g (2 oz) caster (superfine) sugar

300 ml (10 fl oz) thickened (whipping) cream

250 g (9 oz) sour cream

3 tablespoons icing (confectioners') sugar

½ teaspoon almond extract

½ teaspoon vanilla extract

¼ cup (35 g/1¼ oz) crushed pistachio nuts, to serve

Place the apricots, saffron and caster sugar in a small saucepan and cover with 2 cups (500 ml/17 fl oz) water. Bring to a simmer, cover and simmer for 30 minutes until the apricots are softened. Allow to cool to room temperature.

Combine the creams, icing sugar and extracts in a bowl and whip to soft peaks. Fold in the apricots until just combined, reserving a little for layering.

Layer into individual serving dishes and scatter with the pistachios to serve.

Tip

Try this with other fruits, either fresh or dried. A summer version made with fresh berries or peaches would be lovely, as would something more autumnal with quince or dried pears and raisins.

SUPER-SOFT CHOCOLATE MUG CAKE

SERVES 1

Active time
5 minutes

Cooking time
5 minutes

Resting time
30 seconds

Mug cakes can sometimes be a little dry, but this is honestly the softest, ooziest mug cake you'll ever have. The secret is the vegetable oil, which is a fantastic ingredient for baking. Adjust the cooking time to suit your microwave.

½ cup (85 g/3 oz) mug cake mixture (see below)

1 tablespoon vegetable oil

¼ cup (60 ml/2 fl oz) milk

vanilla ice cream, to serve

 MUG CAKE MIXTURE

2 cups (300 g/10½ oz) self-raising (self-rising) flour

2 cups (440 g/15½ oz) caster (superfine) sugar

½ cup (115 g/4 oz) dark brown sugar

1 cup (125 g/4½ oz) Dutch-processed (unsweetened) cocoa powder

1 vanilla bean

Combine the mug cake mixture ingredients in a zip-lock bag and mix to combine. You don't need to split the vanilla bean. It will just perfume the mixture as it sits in your pantry, and you can still use the bean for something else another time – just clean it off.

Combine ½ cup mug cake mixture, vegetable oil and milk in a large mug. Mix to form a batter. Pour in 3 tablespoons boiling water and microwave at 1000W for 90 seconds. Stand for 30 seconds, then serve with vanilla ice cream.

Tip

The dry-ingredient mug cake mixture can be kept in a zip-lock bag in the pantry for months, ready for you to scoop into a mug and mix up a cake at a moment's notice!

SERVES 4

Active time
10 minutes

Cooking time
10 minutes

TOAST SUNDAE

The idea behind this was to make something that played the part of a waffle or pancake, but using bread to avoid the need to make a batter. Honestly, it turned out better than I expected. This was a smash hit.

½ **loaf soft white bread or brioche, unsliced**

75 g (2¾ oz) **unsalted butter, softened**

75 g (2¾ oz) **caster (superfine) sugar**

1 teaspoon **vanilla extract**

fresh berries, to serve

whipped cream, to serve

ice cream, to serve

golden syrup, to serve

Cut the bread into 3 cm (1¼ in) thick slices. Mix the butter, sugar and vanilla together and spread generously over one side of each bread slice, all the way to the edge.

Heat a large frying pan over medium heat and fry the bread, butter-down, until golden. When nearly ready to flip, lightly butter the other side of the bread, all the way to the edge. Flip the bread and cook until golden on the other side. Serve topped with the berries, whipped cream and ice cream, and drizzle with the golden syrup.

Tip

A variation of this is to mix some ground cinnamon into the butter mixture to give you cinnamon toast. It can also be grilled instead of cooked in a pan if you find that easier.

MAKES 20 COOKIES

Active time
15 minutes

Cooking time
15 minutes

Freezing time
2 hours

- 1 cup (250 g/9 oz) unsalted butter, softened
- 200 g (7 oz) soft brown sugar, packed
- 150 g (5½ oz) sugar
- 2 eggs
- 2 teaspoons vanilla extract
- 350 g (12½ oz) plain (all-purpose) flour
- 2 teaspoons bicarbonate of soda (baking soda)
- 1 cup (155 g/5½ oz) toasted almonds, roughly chopped
- 1 cup (150 g/5½ oz) chopped dark chocolate
- 1 tablespoon sea salt flakes

Tip

The dough will spread much more when it's thawed, so if you're intending to bake these from frozen, pressing down the top of each ball before freezing will give you a slightly flatter shape.

ANYTIME CHOCOLATE AND ALMOND COOKIES

Imagine having access to soft, warm, freshly baked cookies at any time of the day or night? With balls of this frozen dough in the freezer, that dream can become a reality.

Combine the butter and sugars in the bowl of a stand mixer fitted with the paddle attachment and beat for 5 minutes until pale and fluffy. Lightly beat the eggs and vanilla together and add, a little a time, to the butter mixture. Sift in the flour and bicarbonate of soda and mix on low speed until combined. Fold through the almond and chocolate.

Line one or two baking trays that will fit in your freezer with baking paper. Using an ice cream scoop, scoop evenly sized balls of the dough and place them on the baking paper. Scatter the balls with salt, gently pressing the salt into each ball to slightly flatten. Freeze for 2 hours until firm. Transfer to a large zip-lock bag and freeze until needed.

To bake the cookies, heat your oven to 180°C (360°F) fan-forced and line a baking tray with baking paper. Place any amount of cookies you'd like to cook on the prepared baking tray and bake for 12 minutes until just starting to brown around the edges. Cool for 5 minutes and serve warm.

INDEX

A
almonds: Anytime chocolate and almond cookies 13, 215
Aloo matar with brown butter tadka 54
'Antipasta' 161
Anytime chocolate and almond cookies 13, 215
apples: Blue cheese and green apple salad 40
Apricot and sour cream fool 208
asparagus: Beef, asparagus and capsicum 187
Assiette de crudités 37

B
bacon
    Bacon and corn croutons 59
    Carbonara fried rice 33
    Edamame succotash 63
    Frozen pea soup with bacon and corn croutons 59
    Pan-roasted flathead with peas, greens and bacon 103
    Salad Lyonnaise 22
    see also pancetta, speck
Baked rice pudding with plum jam 207
Baked Tuscan chicken 127
Barbecued squid with oregano and paprika 112
Basic vinaigrette 13, 37
beans
    Kidney bean curry 46
    see also green beans
beef
    Beef, asparagus and capsicum 187
    Beef pad prik khing 177
    Beef pad see ew 190
    Beef tagliata 78
    Cheeseburger sang choy bao 86
    Rump cap with quick chimichurri 74
    Swedish mince 80
blue cheese
    Blue cheese and green apple salad 40
    Fisherman's lunch 34
Bombay cheese toast 30
bread
    Bombay cheese toast 30
    Dakos toast 39
    Frozen pea soup with bacon and corn croutons 59
    Ricotta eggs on toast 64
    The original caesar salad 29
    Toast sundae 212
    Tomato tartine 25
butter
    Aloo matar with brown butter tadka 54
    Kimchi and garlic butter fried rice 57
    Whole baked fish with vadouvan butter 137
Buttered new potatoes 83

C
cabbage: Shanghai shredded pork and cabbage 172
cake
    Mug cake mixture 13, 210
    Super-soft chocolate mug cake 210
Cantonese sweet soy sauce 13, 184
capsicums
    Assiette de crudités 37
    Beef, asparagus and capsicum 187
    Edamame succotash 63

Mushroom cacciatore 133
Tomato and capsicum penne 146
Carbonara fried rice 33
Carrot and green bean stew 53
cheese
Blue cheese and green apple salad 40
Bombay cheese toast 30
Cheeseburger sang choy bao 86
Chicken and cream cheese penne 152
Dakos toast 39
Fisherman's lunch 34
Ricotta eggs on toast 64
see also blue cheese, feta
chicken
Baked Tuscan chicken 127
Chicken and choy sum 183
Chicken and cream cheese penne 152
Chicken and snow peas with oyster sauce 178
Creamy chicken, leek and mushroom stew 130
Crumbed chicken tenders with pesto mayonnaise 104
Garlic chicken drumsticks 88
Hawaiian shoyu chicken 141
Honey mustard chicken cutlets 134
Orange and fennel chicken traybake 122
Quick chicken noodles 98
Soy sauce chicken with spring onion oil 138
Three-cup chicken 175
Turkish tandoori drumsticks 77
chimichurri
Quick chimichurri 13, 74
Rump cap with quick chimichurri 74
chocolate
Anytime chocolate and almond cookies 13, 215
Chocolate granita 196
Super-soft chocolate mug cake 210
choy sum: Chicken and choy sum 183
convenience foods 9, 10, 12–13
Colcannon risotto 125
cookies: Anytime chocolate and almond cookies 13, 215
corn
Bacon and corn croutons 59
Edamame succotash 63

Frozen pea soup with bacon and corn croutons 59
cream
Baked Tuscan chicken 127
Creamy chicken, leek and mushroom stew 130
Creamy lemon pasta 165
Paccheri with pancetta and pistachio 149
Vanilla cream 199
see also sour cream
Crumbed chicken tenders with pesto mayonnaise 104
curry
Curried egg furikake 26
Curried furikake 13, 26
Dukra maas 120
Kerala egg curry 51
Kidney bean curry 46
Mangalorean pork masala 120
Quick Sri Lankan prawn curry 115

D

Dakos toast 39
Decaffogato 205
desserts
Apricot and sour cream fool 208
Baked rice pudding with plum jam 207
Chocolate granita 196
Decaffogato 205
Kaiserschmarrn 201
Mug cake mixture 13, 210
Scrambled pancakes 201
Super-soft chocolate mug cake 210
Toast sundae 212
Weet-Bix mille-feuille 199
dressings: Basic vinaigrette 13, 37
duck: Quick duck à l'orange with sarladaise potatoes 107
Dukra maas 120

E

Edamame succotash 63
eggs
Carbonara fried rice 33
Curried egg furikake 26
Fried eggs and soy sauce 184

Kerala egg curry 51
Kimchi and garlic butter fried rice 57
Prawns and eggs 171
Ricotta eggs on toast 64
Salad Lyonnaise 22
Tamago-don 60

F
fennel
    Orange and fennel chicken traybake 122
    Stir-fried pork and fennel 189
feta: Dakos toast 39
fish
    Fisherman's lunch 34
    Pan-roasted flathead with peas, greens and bacon 103
    Pasta alla carlofortina 158
    Salmon with parsley and dill sauce 101
    Steamed flathead with spinach and lemon sauce 111
    Tinned fish with capers and tomato spaghetti 155
    Whole baked fish with vadouvan butter 137
    see also flathead, salmon
flathead
    Pan-roasted flathead with peas, greens and bacon 103
    Steamed flathead with spinach and lemon sauce 111
Fried eggs and soy sauce 184
Frozen pea soup with bacon and corn croutons 59
Frozen vegetable fried rice 71

G
Gambas al ajillo 109
garlic
    Garlic chicken drumsticks 88
    Kimchi and garlic butter fried rice 57
granita: Chocolate granita 196
green beans
    Beef pad prik khing 177
    Carrot and green bean stew 53
Greens 125

H
Hawaiian shoyu chicken 141
Herb ranch 85
Honey mustard chicken cutlets 134

K
Kaiserschmarrn 201
Kerala egg curry 51
Kidney bean curry 46
Kimchi and garlic butter fried rice 57
knife skills 15, 68–9

L
lamb
    Lamb kheema 91
    Turkish roast lamb shoulder 129
lemon
    Creamy lemon pasta 165
    Prawn and lemon guazzetto 96
    Spinach and lemon sauce 111
    Steamed flathead with spinach and lemon sauce 111
lettuce
    Beef tagliata 78
    Blue cheese and green apple salad 40
    Cheeseburger sang choy bao 86
    Little French peas 48
    Petits pois à la Française 48
    Salad Lyonnaise 22
    The original caesar salad 29
    Tomato tartine 25
Linguine with mussels and pancetta 157
Little French peas 48

M
Mangalorean pork masala 120
Masala chai 202
Mashed potato 80
mayonnaise
    Crumbed chicken tenders with pesto mayonnaise 104
    Fisherman's lunch 34
    Herb ranch 85
    Sour cream and dill sauce 34
Mint yoghurt 129

Mug cake mixture 13, 210
mushrooms
    Creamy chicken, leek and mushroom stew 130
    Mushroom cacciatore 133
    Seafood yakisoba 181
    Tamago-don 60
mussels: Linguine with mussels and pancetta 157
mustard
    Honey mustard chicken cutlets 134
    Sausages in cider and mustard 83

N

noodles
    Beef pad see ew 190
    Quick chicken noodles 98
    Seafood yakisoba 181

O

oils
    Smoked paprika oil 13, 146
    Spring onion oil 13, 138
olives
    'Antipasta' 161
    Dakos toast 39
onions
    Honey mustard chicken cutlets 134
    Little French peas 48
    Orange and fennel chicken traybake 122
    Petits pois à la Française 48
    Roast pumpkin with tahini sauce 73
    Sausages in cider and mustard 83
    Sumac onions 129
orange
    Orange and fennel chicken traybake 122
    Orange sauce 107
    Quick duck à l'orange with sarladaise potatoes 107

P

Paccheri with pancetta and pistachio 149
Pad see ew sauce 190
pancakes: Scrambled pancakes 201
pancetta
    Linguine with mussels and pancetta 157
    Paccheri with pancetta and pistachio 149
    see also bacon, speck
Pan-roasted flathead with peas, greens and bacon 103
Pantry pasta 162
pasta
    'Antipasta' 161
    Chicken and cream cheese penne 152
    Creamy lemon pasta 165
    Linguine with mussels and pancetta 157
    Paccheri with pancetta and pistachio 149
    Pantry pasta 162
    Pasta alla carlofortina 158
    Spaghetti vongole rosso 151
    Tinned fish with capers and tomato spaghetti 155
    Tomato and capsicum penne 146
peas
    Aloo matar with brown butter tadka 54
    Chicken and cream cheese penne 152
    Frozen pea soup with bacon and corn croutons 59
    Lamb kheema 91
    Little French peas 48
    Pan-roasted flathead with peas, greens and bacon 103
Petits pois à la Française 48
Polenta 133
pork
    Dukra maas 120
    Mangalorean pork masala 120
    Shanghai shredded pork and cabbage 172
    Stir-fried pork and fennel 189
    Swedish mince 80
potatoes
    Aloo matar with brown butter tadka 54
    Barbecued squid with oregano and paprika 112
    Buttered new potatoes 83
    Mashed potato 80
    Quick duck à l'orange with sarladaise potatoes 107
    Sarladaise potatoes 107
    Twice-roasted potatoes 13, 85

prawns
    Frozen vegetable fried rice 71
    Gambas al ajillo 109
    Prawn and lemon guazzetto 96
    Prawns and eggs 171
    Quick Sri Lankan prawn curry 115
    Seafood yakisoba 181
    Spanish garlic prawns 109
pumpkin: Roast pumpkin with tahini sauce 73

Q

Quick chicken noodles 98
Quick chimichurri 13, 74
Quick duck à l'orange with sarladaise potatoes 107
Quick Sri Lankan prawn curry 115

R

rice
    Baked rice pudding with plum jam 207
    Carbonara fried rice 33
    Colcannon risotto 125
    Frozen vegetable fried rice 71
    Kimchi and garlic butter fried rice 57
    Tamago-don 60
Ricotta eggs on toast 64
risotto: Colcannon risotto 125
Roast pumpkin with tahini sauce 73
Rump cap with quick chimichurri 74

S

salads
    Blue cheese and green apple salad 40
    Salad Lyonnaise 22
    The original caesar salad 29
salmon
    Fisherman's lunch 34
    Salmon with parsley and dill sauce 101
Sarladaise potatoes 107
Salted yoghurt 53
sauces
    Cantonese sweet soy sauce 13, 184
    Chicken and snow peas with oyster sauce 178
    Crumbed chicken tenders with pesto mayonnaise 104
    Herb ranch 85
    Pad see ew sauce 190
    Roast pumpkin with tahini sauce 73
    Sour cream and dill sauce 34
    Soy sauce braise (lo sui) 13, 138
    Spinach and lemon sauce 111
    Steamed flathead with spinach and lemon sauce 111
    Yakisoba sauce 13, 181
Sausages in cider and mustard 83
Scrambled pancakes 201
seafood
    Barbecued squid with oregano and paprika 112
    Frozen vegetable fried rice 71
    Gambas al ajillo 109
    Linguine with mussels and pancetta 157
    Prawn and lemon guazzetto 96
    Prawns and eggs 171
    Quick Sri Lankan prawn curry 115
    Seafood yakisoba 181
    Spaghetti vongole rosso 151
    Spanish garlic prawns 109
seasonings
    Curried furikake 13, 26
    Vadouvan curry powder 13, 137
Shanghai shredded pork and cabbage 172
Smoked paprika oil 13, 146
snow peas: Chicken and snow peas with oyster sauce 178
soups
    Frozen pea soup with bacon and corn croutons 59
sour cream
    Apricot and sour cream fool 208
    Sour cream and dill sauce 34
soy sauce
    Cantonese sweet soy sauce 13, 184
    Fried eggs and soy sauce 184
    Soy sauce chicken with spring onion oil 138
    Soy sauce braise (lo sui) 13, 138
Spaghetti vongole rosso 151
Spanish garlic prawns 109

speck: Little French peas 48
   see also bacon, pancetta
Spinach and lemon sauce 111
spring onions
   Hawaiian shoyu chicken 141
   Soy sauce chicken with spring onion oil 138
   Spring onion oil 13, 138
squid: Barbecued squid with oregano and paprika 112
Steamed flathead with spinach and lemon sauce 111
stews
   Carrot and green bean stew 53
   Creamy chicken, leek and mushroom stew 130
stir-fries
   Beef, asparagus and capsicum 187
   Beef pad prik khing 177
   Beef pad see ew 190
   Chicken and choy sum 183
   Chicken and snow peas with oyster sauce 178
   Prawns and eggs 171
   Seafood yakisoba 181
   Shanghai shredded pork and cabbage 172
   Stir-fried pork and fennel 189
   Three-cup chicken 175
Sumac onions 129
Super-soft chocolate mug cake 210
Swedish mince 80

T

Tadka 54
Tamago-don 60
The original caesar salad 29
Three-cup chicken 175
time-saving tips 14–5
Tinned fish with capers and tomato spaghetti 155
Toast sundae 212
tomatoes
   'Antipasta' 161
   Edamame succotash 63
   Pantry pasta 162
   Pasta alla carlofortina 158
   Prawn and lemon guazzetto 96
   Tinned fish with capers and tomato spaghetti 155
   Tomato and capsicum penne 146
   Tomato tartine 25
Turkish roast lamb shoulder 129
Turkish tandoori drumsticks 77
Twice-roasted potatoes 13, 85

V

vadouvan
   Vadouvan curry powder 13, 137
   Whole baked fish with vadouvan butter 137
Vanilla cream 199
vinaigrette: Basic vinaigrette 13, 37
vongole
   Seafood yakisoba 181
   Spaghetti vongole rosso 151

W

Weet-Bix mille-feuille 199
Whole baked fish with vadouvan butter 137
Wok-cooking 168–9

Y

Yakisoba sauce 13, 181
yoghurt
   Mint yoghurt 129
   Salted yoghurt 53
   Turkish tandoori drumsticks 77

Index 221

ABOUT ADAM

Adam Liaw thinks cooking is important. As a busy father of three who cooks for his family (nearly) every night, he understands the challenges of the evening meal but he also appreciates the daily joy that it can bring.

He believes that dinner is more than just food on a plate. It's an occasion that brings us together and sets the scene for our relationships, health and happiness ... and it doesn't have to be complicated.

Adam is the No. 1 food writer for *Good Food* in *The Sydney Morning Herald* and *The Age*, and SBS Food. He's also the long-running weekly food columnist for *Sunday Life* magazine.

On television he is the host of *The Cook Up with Adam Liaw*, SBS's largest-ever television commission, now in its seventh season. He also hosts *Good Food Kitchen*, the award-winning *Destination Flavour* series and many other food and documentary programs.

Adam is UNICEF Australia's National Ambassador for Nutrition.

Time for Dinner is his tenth cookbook.

THANK YOU

Years ago when we started making *The Cook Up*, we made a very simple but deliberate decision to remove ego from guiding our decisions. If there was something we could do to help people with their cooking, we'd choose that road. If there was a simpler way to make a dish, we'd do it.

Hundreds of episodes later, that decision has proven to be our greatest asset.

It put you – our audience – at the centre of what we do. It's given us a purpose and a direction to keep striving to make our show more informative, more entertaining and more useful to all of you.

Decisions like that aren't the easiest to make. It has meant we've had to make some sacrifices but our team has done this day in, day out for years now.

I'd like to express my constant gratitude to Emily Griggs, Damien McDermott, Gavin Jarrett, Alex Cassimaty, Kate Nicholls and Vanessa Miles, who keep making *The Cook Up* better and better every single day we walk into the room.

To the whole team at *The Cook Up*: cameras, sound, the floor, the back of house, the control room, HMU, lighting, editing, production … the list is endless. There's a reason every guest that walks out of the studio is full of praise for everything you do, and I couldn't agree more.

To the excellent publishing team at Hardie Grant who never shy from the task of taking hundreds of episodes of television made by hundreds of people and distilling it down to something you can hold in your hand. Simon Davis, Claire Davis, Roxy Ryan, George Saad and more, thank you for the trust you continue to give me and for helping wrestle this difficult beast onto the page.

To my manager, Melita Hodge, who helps me steer this ship every day.

And last but not least, a huge thank you to the most reliable team of Steve Brown, Bernadette Smithies, Olivia Andrews and Kay Wijaya. I can barely count the number of projects we've all worked on together over the years, and it just gets more and more fun every time.

Published in 2024 by Hardie Grant Books,
an imprint of Hardie Grant Publishing

Hardie Grant Books (Melbourne)
Wurundjeri Country
Building 1, 658 Church Street
Richmond, Victoria 3121

Hardie Grant North America
2912 Telegraph Ave
Berkeley, California 94705

hardiegrant.com/books

Hardie Grant acknowledges the Traditional Owners of the Country on which we work, the Wurundjeri People of the Kulin Nation and the Gadigal People of the Eora Nation, and recognises their continuing connection to the land, waters and culture. We pay our respects to their Elders past and present.

All rights reserved. No part of this publication may be reproduced, stored in a retrieval system or transmitted in any form by any means, electronic, mechanical, photocopying, recording or otherwise, without the prior written permission of the publishers and copyright holders.

The moral rights of the author have been asserted.

Copyright text © Adam Liaw 2024
Copyright photography © Steve Brown 2024
Copyright design © Hardie Grant Publishing 2024

A catalogue record for this book is available from the National Library of Australia

Time for Dinner
ISBN 978 1 74379 979 6
ISBN 978 1 76144 162 2 (ebook)

10 9 8 7 6 5 4 3 2 1

Publisher: Simon Davis
Head of Editorial: Jasmin Chua
Project Editor: Claire Davis
Editor: Pru Engel
Design Manager: Kristin Thomas
Designer: George Saad
Typesetter: Hannah Schubert
Photographer: Steve Brown
Stylist (internals): Bernadette Smithies
Stylist (cover): Vanessa Austin
Home Economists: Kay Wijaya, Olivia Andrews
Head of Production: Todd Rechner
Production Controller: Jessica Harvie

Colour reproduction by Splitting Image Colour Studio
Printed in China by Leo Paper Products LTD.

The paper this book is printed on is from FSC®-certified forests and other sources. FSC® promotes environmentally responsible, socially beneficial and economically viable management of the world's forests.